When Moses Meets Aaron

When Moses Meets Aaron

Staffing and Supervision in Large Congregations

Gil Rendle and Susan Beaumont

THE
ALBAN
INSTITUTE
Hermdon, Virginia
www.alban.org

The Alban Institute
2121 Cooperative Way, Suite 100
Herndon, VA 20171

Library of Congress Cataloging-in-Publication Data

Rendle, Gilbert R.
  When Moses meets Aaron : staffing and supervision in large congregations / Gil Rendle and Susan Beaumont.
    p. cm.
  Includes bibliographical references.
  ISBN 978-1-56699-351-7
  1. Church personnel management. 2. Christian leadership. 3. Church management. 4. Supervision of employees. 5. Big churches. I. Beaumont, Susan II. Title.

  BV652.13.R46 2007
  254—dc22

                              2007027477

    12   11   10   09   08   UG   2   3   4   5   6

*In memory of my father, Norm Allen, whose quiet strength
shaped my understanding of leadership.*
—S.B.

For Lynne—love, laughter, and life.
—G.R.

Contents

Introduction

Why a Book of Resources for Leading Staff

A Quick History

The large congregation is a relatively new development. In a study of megachurches (congregations with average attendance at worship of two thousand or more people) done by the Hartford Institute for Religion Research, only 6 such congregations existed at the beginning of the twentieth century. By 1960 there were only 16. The number of these largest congregations began to grow in the 1970s, and by 2005 there were 1,210 megachurches in the United States representing independent, evangelical, and mainline congregations.[1] Clearly something is happening.

This is not a book about megachurches. They are, however, a bellwether of the recent explosion of large congregations that has every indication of continuing in a culture that appreciates and tends to gravitate toward large institutions. One of the consequences of this rapid growth in the number of large congregations is a lack of training and tools available for senior clergy to lead these large congregations.

From the beginning until recent years, American religion has been a small congregation experience. Denominations began with small congregations being planted in towns, villages, and hamlets to take the faith to neighborhoods and crossroads where people lived. What developed was a very large number of small congregations serving very few people. Of the estimated 350,000 congregations in the United States today (Protestant, Catholic, and Jewish) a full 50 percent of them currently provide ministry to only 11 percent of the people who are involved with congregations.[2] We have many,

1

many congregations with small memberships, family dynamics, and relational leaders. This is the milieu in which seminaries and denominations have learned to train, deploy, and evaluate their clergy. Even today the average attendance across all congregations in the United States is only seventy-five people.[3] So it is natural that the preparation and resourcing of senior leaders of today's large congregations are behind the curve. It has taken seminaries and denominations some time to realize that something new was needed.

A part of our delay in responding has been caused by a cultural shift in generational values that hid some of the changes now facing congregations. For while the largest of the congregations may be a very new phenomenon, we have always had midsize and moderately large congregations. In addition, we have memory that easily recalls pastors of those earlier somewhat large congregations who managed well with the same training and tools as everyone else. As recently as twenty-five to thirty years ago, it was possible to pastor a congregation with an average worship attendance of five hundred people with no or only part-time programmatic staff to help. Gil grew up in a congregation where between five hundred and seven hundred people worshiped, depending on the season. When he was a child, the church had only a solo full-time pastor. By the time he was in high school, the church staff had grown by only one additional clergy so that the church had a senior pastor and an assistant youth pastor.

Moderate to large congregations with solo pastors or only modest program staff were possible then because of the cultural values and consensus of membership. It was a time of "group" values in which personal identity was shaped by the groups one belonged to, and it was culturally assumed that if a person joined a group, he or she was in agreement with and willing to support that group's programs and practices. Another way of expressing this is to say that it was a time of cultural consensus among members of established organizations. It made sense then for a congregation to have few staff, because clergy were leading people who already agreed on what the congregation would do and who were ready to self-organize to make the assumed programs happen. With few staff and an already established consensus in the membership, clergy needed and used few organizational skills beyond relational leadership.

Large congregations today are different from those of years gone by and have learned to do ministry in a very different culture. Today our large congregations (350 or more people in average attendance at worship) are culturally attractive and in a number of denominations are responsible for the greatest percentage of ministry with people. For instance, in the United Methodist denomination, the largest two hundred congregations represent only 0.5 percent of all congregations in that denomination. However, the members of those two hundred congregations represent a full 9.5 percent of all United Methodists in the United States.[4] Our large congregations are not only greater in size but also in complexity and in their capacity to do ministry with persons across great personal and institutional differences.

Following are a few of the characteristics of large congregations often pointed to that make them "culturally comfortable" and able to do ministry in the current cultural setting:

Choice. Large congregations offer members and participants many options of involvement and opportunities to support their spiritual development. People can choose what is most meaningful and helpful in their lives without having to "buy the whole package." Only in the last few decades has worship itself become a program choice—an option in a person's involvement with their faith that they can take or leave.

Anonymity. Large congregations not only offer choices but allow people not to choose and have their nonparticipation go without notice. In a large congregation it is easy and acceptable to be involved only in what is most meaningful to the individual. Being a "good" member or participant does not require sitting on committees, supporting all efforts and programs, or giving time or dollars beyond levels personally determined. In large congregations people can get deeply involved in small groups and in meaningful programs and still remain anonymous to the rest of the organization. This provides a real advantage to people in an overcommitted culture with little discretionary time left over in any given day or week.

Diversity. Large congregations are broadly diverse in both obvious (race, age, gender) and subtle (socioeconomic, theological, political) ways. Such diversity is widely appreciated by the people involved in large congregations. It is also somewhat unique. Few other organizations in the current culture routinely invite people to gather together across their "market segment" differences to form community. The secret of the large congregation is that people are invited to appreciate and participate in diversity without having to negotiate it. A participant can sit in worship and marvel at all of the differences that surround her, but following worship she is free to move on to the mission group or the small study group where the people are much more like her in shared interests and values if not in lifestyle. The clergy, staff, and governing boards in large congregations are responsible for dealing with the wide range of personal preferences and competing demands that come with diversity.

Today the changed realities surrounding large congregations make them increasingly complex organizations. The complexity stems from an environment, both internally among members and participants and externally in a segmenting and targeting culture, where multiple preferences, expectations, and needs live side by side. Large congregations no longer unite around relationships but around clear missions and goals. Senior clergy need to be skilled with the tools of visioning and mission development so that competing preferences and needs can be negotiated, connected, and aligned at the center of the mission of the congregation. Large congregations are now dependent on a larger number of staff to meet the distinct and competing needs of an increasingly diverse assembly of members and participants. Senior clergy need to be skilled with the tools of human resource management to align the efforts and outputs of staff with the central mission of the congregation. Working without adequate models and tools, senior clergy often find themselves with passionate, dedicated staff members who are moving in different directions, competing over limited resources and attention. They end up with questions of how to evaluate the performance of staff and direct their efforts. They find themselves using time, attention, and resources to care for staff rather than using staff as a resource to care for the mission of the congregation.

This book of resources for senior clergy leading staff is a contribution to support the changing need in large congregations for leadership models and tools. We discuss theories within these pages because there is power in ideas and it matters what we think and what we assume as leaders. We identify principles and practices that allow for—and require—adaptation. Although large congregations have much in common, they are also individually unique with differing organizational or communal cultures and histories that make one-size-fits-all approaches unhelpful. We include actual examples of "best practices" because there is much we can learn from one another. Undergirding all of this, you will find a deeply held assumption that congregations are valuable and precious in God's sight. It is in congregations that truly renewable resources—the resources of the human spirit and the resource of the Spirit of God—can find one another and be replenished again and again in life-giving ways.

PART 1

A Framework for Thinking about Employment Relationships

Chapter 1

People Are Resources for Ministry

Look at Moses. You will see that leading a complex enterprise and managing people are about much more than organizational effectiveness and excellence and certainly about more than tidiness and keeping people happy. Leadership needs to be concerned with faithfulness and stewardship of the resources necessary to accomplish the goals and vision of ministry. Getting out of Egypt and across the Red Sea was not easy for the Israelites. Moses was obviously a primary player in that chapter of history, and the vision of the Promised Land clearly drew the people forward. To get to the fulfilled vision, however, Moses and the other leaders faced a vast wilderness and a seemingly endless list of challenges and tasks to manage.

Like many high-profile leaders, Moses began to do too much. Perhaps it was a carryover from the centrality of his role in Egypt. No one person, however, can know all the steps toward a vision, possess all the skills needed to get there, and have the endurance to provide the energy to move forward continually. It took Moses's father-in-law, Jethro, to pull an exhausted Moses aside, help him assign the appropriate work to others, and provide the organizational/community structure that would sustain the energy needed for travel. It took the two brothers, Moses and Aaron, just to get the primary needs of the vision (Moses's responsibility) and the community (Aaron's responsibility) met. The first lesson in leadership was about sharing it.

A rabbi friend once shared with Gil a wonderful contemporary midrash about leadership (vision) and management (administration). The midrash speaks of Moses as the voice of *leadership* for the Israelites. It was Moses who went apart to speak with God and who returned with a glowing face and new insight into the future of God's people. Aaron was the voice of *management* to complement Moses's leadership. It was Aaron who organized the journey and met the more immediate needs of the people. The midrash points out that it is essential but not sufficient simply to provide both leadership and management. Of equal importance is keeping leadership and management connected and aligned. When Moses was on top of the mountain receiving the commandments, he was separated by too much distance from Aaron, who was at that very moment at the base of the mountain breaking one of the commandments. While casting an idol seemed expedient to Aaron, it was in opposition to the vision Moses received of being a people who were faithful to the one true God. If the first lesson was sharing leadership, the second lesson was about alignment and connections.

Shared leadership and alignment of efforts is all about people and the way they are connected and directed in the work of the congregation. In writing about people (human resource) management, business educators Eliza Collins and Mary Anne Devanna note that "few managerial processes offer the opportunity to leverage employee behavior and organizational performance as effectively as the human resource function. Yet human resource management continues to occupy very little of the manager's time and attention."[1]

People Are Resources

Because ministry is about people, we often neglect seeing people themselves as resources for ministry. People, of course, are the *recipients* of ministry, and a changed person is often the *goal* of ministry. But ministry is done by people who also need to be seen as a primary *resource* for doing ministry

The confusion about people being either resources or goals can often be seen when a congregation stretches its vision in a way that requires the addition of a new staff person. To take the step of increasing staff, money often needs to be raised and new structures may need to be put in place. When the new staff person finally is identified and begins work, there is great celebration and a sense of accomplishment. Then the level of energy and activity often settles down and little new happens. At the heart of the inactivity and lack of change is confusion over resources and goals. The new staff person commonly is mistaken for the goal. When the new person is put in place, it feels right for leaders to check the task of increasing staff off their to-do list and settle back to life as usual.

The problem is that the new staff person isn't being recognized as a *resource* needed to address *some other goal* of ministry. For example, the goal of the congregation is not to hire a new youth minister, but to provide or to increase ministry with youth—for which it is determined that the resource of a new youth minister is needed. Likewise, the goal of the congregation is not to hire an additional music director with skills in contemporary worship, but to provide worship that speaks to and meets the needs of people who do not respond well to traditional worship—for which a music director with contemporary skills is needed.

A difficult transition for senior clergy and congregational personnel committees is to recognize staff and leaders (clergy or lay, paid or volunteer, full-time or part-time) as resources, not goals, as providers, not recipients, of ministry. Schooled in pastoral care and community support, senior clergy and personnel committees mistake their role as being caregivers to the people who are called forth as employees or volunteers to lead the ministry of the congregation. Consider the congregation that accepted the reduction of a staff member's hours (without commensurate reduction in salary) because the staff member found it difficult to provide child care. Or the congregation that was reluctant to mention the associate pastor's absences and failure to complete work assignments because he was "having a difficult time at home." Of course, in faith communities we need to be careful and responsible in our relationships with others—coworkers included. Workers, however, need to be seen by senior clergy and personnel committees as resources for, rather than recipients of, ministry. Like all resources, they need to be stewarded, directed, aligned, supervised, and used with account-ability. Organizationally this function of leadership is known as *human resource management*.

It is widely acknowledged that clergy, who are expected to provide primary leadership and management to congregations, are not well prepared for the task of human resource management. Identifying some contributing factors is fairly easy:

- Professional training typically focuses on the disciplines of the profession itself. Running a law office or managing a medical practice requires another complete body of business knowledge and experience that lawyers or physicians must either learn or purchase to support their primary practice. Such training is not sufficiently provided in their professional preparation. In like ways, the seminary offers preparation for ministry, not for congregational leadership and people management.

- The performance of ministry has a long tradition of taking the form of "lone ranger" leadership, in which congregations practice clergy dependence (and scapegoating) by believing that all ministry is up to the clergy. Clergy often collude by trying to do it all.

- The growth in the number of large congregations that need multiple staff members—and therefore more formal practices of staff management—is a relatively new cultural experience. Attention to developing a leadership skill set related to human resource management was not previously needed or well regarded in congregations.

- Having an abundance of resources (primarily dollars and volunteers) does not encourage or require learning how to manage or steward resources. This is easily seen in settings where leaders manage their problems by "throwing money at the problems" because they have the money to throw. Established congregations come from an earlier American cultural background in which people's time (like money in an expanding economy) seemed like an inexhaustible resource. Members were expected to give hours, days, and weeks to participation and leadership in their congregation. Leaders today, however, are providing ministry with and to people with a rapidly decreasing amount of discretionary time and who experience a vastly expanded competition as to how they will use that discretionary time. People's commitment to their faith or their congregation can no longer be measured by the amount of time they give. As discretionary time shrinks, leaders have to learn how to use volunteer time more effectively, replace volunteer hours with staff hours, and manage staff as a costly and limited resource.

A number of years ago, a highly regarded and high-profile senior clergy of a large metropolitan congregation took a newly hired staff person out to lunch during her first week as the new minister of community outreach. Anticipating that she would learn much more of what was expected from her by the senior clergy, the new associate was shocked by the pleasant but general luncheon conversation about the church and community. The senior clergy ended the luncheon by wishing her well in figuring out what she would do as minister of outreach. This was management by hope—hope that the senior clergy would not have to get involved. What is needed today in our changed environment is greater, but appropriate, engagement by senior leaders that requires new learning and intentional practices of supervision of staff in congregations.

How You Think Matters

Before moving too quickly to skills and practices, it is important to remember that what we do is influenced and directed by what we believe and how we think. Organizational leadership in a congregation is a spiritual task because it is the acting out of what we believe about ourselves, about people, and about how we use ourselves for God's purpose.

How You Think about Yourself Matters

On the one hand is the tenacious image of the lone ranger, the singular leader who can tell others what to do and how to do it.

As our organizations and congregations have increasingly become more complex and as the number of large multistaff congregations has grown, the lone ranger has not disappeared simply because he or she is no longer alone.

Jim Collins, author and lecturer who provides management research for companies of excellence, identifies in larger organizations the "genius with a thousand helpers" model, which is the image of a singular leader in a large organization.[2] The lone ranger may now have a host of Tontos, but leadership still lies primarily with the lone ranger. Collins argues that the "genius with a thousand helpers" as a leadership model is particularly prevalent in organizations that are unable to sustain excellence. The life and effectiveness of the organization with a singular leader are limited by:

- the singular leader's need to be in charge and in control, which limits the participation of others
- the leader's assumption that he or she must know all the "answers," thereby cutting short the creativity and imagination of others
- the lack of communication among staff who resist sharing all that they are working on because of the overcontrol of the leader, which requires that all of their ideas and actions be filtered through the leader's approval and direction
- the leader's exhaustion from trying to do his or her own work while simultaneously needing to direct the work of others
- the leader's diminished feelings of self-worth when, as resident "genius," he or she cannot give clear directions because the work requires new learning that exceeds the gifts and passions of the leader

On the other hand—in contrast to the familiar lone ranger—are models of supervision and leadership in which the senior leader is not the primary "doer" with multiple helpers, but takes responsibility to help and resource others as they work toward the organization's mission. The image that Marcus Buckingham and Curt Coffman, consultants and lecturers with the Gallup Organization, use in their

discussion of great managers is that of catalyst: "As with all cata-
lysts, the manager's function is to speed up the reaction between two
substances, thus creating the desired end product. Specifically the
manager creates performance in each employee by speeding up the
reaction between the employee's talents and the company's goals,
and between the employee's talents and the customer's need."[3]

The work of the leader as catalyst supports the effective work
of others, as well as the personal and professional development of
others by:

- giving the work to the people to whom it belongs
- giving attention to the resources that others need to do
  their work
- removing the barriers that limit the work and effectiveness
  of others
- being a conversation partner where creative new ideas and
  learning can be spawned
- keeping the work of the staff aligned with the intended
  outcomes and mission of the organization so that efforts
  are not diluted or misdirected

How the leader thinks about himself or herself matters for more
than organizational reasons. There is a large spiritual question here,
as well. Does the way in which leaders think of themselves as leaders allow room for God? Once while serving as senior pastor of an
urban congregation and showing obvious symptoms of overwork,
Gil was taken aside by Harrell Beck, professor of Hebrew wisdom
literature at Boston University School of Theology. More than a
teacher, Beck was also a friend and mentor. He was direct and
scolding as he talked about his disappointment that Gil had forgot-
ten the difference between prophetic eschatology and apocalyptic
eschatology. Responding to what must have been a blank expression, Beck reminded Gil that the prophets never expected that the
end would come by action of their own hand. They had a role to
play in announcing God's presence and intent, but they always left
plenty of room for God to do what they could not. There were
times when a prophet could be surprised—or even disappointed,

like Jonah—by how much God could do. By taking up too much of a role, the leader can diminish the space allowed for God. When a leader assumes that what is needed is a hero, he or she has a hard lesson to learn.

How You Think about Others and Their Work Matters

In a pivotal book, *The Human Side of Enterprise*[4] published in 1960, organizational consultant Douglas McGregor set the terms for future conversations about the relationship between leaders and workers by offering two contrasting assumptions about workers—identified as Theory X and Theory Y.

Theory X assumes that people are essentially lazy, irresponsible, passive, and dependent on the leader who must be able to break work down into manageable pieces and then direct, control, evaluate, and motivate the workers to make them productive. Under Theory X, the leader's role is pivotal and the leader's responsibility is extensive since the workers will produce little without the direct involvement of the leader.

Theory Y, however, begins with the assumption that people essentially want to do well—that they seek meaning in their work, will take responsibility for their jobs, wish to grow in their work, and willingly seek excellence. Under Theory Y, the leader's role is remarkably different—resourcing rather than directing; challenging; offering both support and accountability rather than evaluation; and often simply getting out of the way.

It matters how you think of others and their work, because Theory X and Theory Y require very different roles and skill sets for the leader. Not to be missed is the significant spiritual question of the worth of the person. Responding to McGregor, Warren Bennis, noted consultant and teacher, stated correctly that what was being offered was two theories of human behavior—each informed by compassion, but one based on essential sinfulness and the other on the potential goodness and strength of each person.[5]

Clearly Theory X and Theory Y are not opposites but are poles on a continuum on which we must find our own place. Where we place ourselves on the continuum of assumptions about others and their work matters. The senior clergy of one large congregation with which Gil worked made a habit of driving past the home of an assistant clergy on his staff. The drives were timed randomly to track when and how often that staff member's car was in his home driveway. The senior clergy would then "confront" this staff person for not working hard enough. Not surprisingly, the staff member was demoralized and self-protective—feeling, if not sinful, at least inadequate. Driving by a staff member's home and having confrontational meetings take time and effort. Consider the differences if that time had been given to making sure that the staff person clearly knew the outcomes expected of his work and was resourced, supported, and given structures of accountability.

How You Think about the Body of Christ Matters

The first letter of Paul to the Corinthians begins with an argument over who the real leader is, who is to be followed. Is it Cephas, Apollos, or Paul? Who is in charge? Who is to be listened to? Paul is clear throughout the letter that whatever the differences among the leaders, they are all spokespersons for Christ. Paul spends time explaining differences, using the idea of spiritual gifts (1 Corinthians 12). There are a variety of gifts, but they are of the same Spirit—just as there are a variety of tasks and responsibilities all in the service of the same God. In that same chapter, Paul goes on to use the metaphor of the body to make a similar point. The body is composed of different parts, all of which are needed but none of which is the whole. In fact, if you are a foot, it is a good idea not to try to behave as a hand. Ideas and metaphors can be continued to make the argument that:

- The reason we have gifts is to serve God and others for the ultimate outcome of glorifying God.
- We all have different gifts, including the leader.
- No one has all the gifts, including the leader.
- Like the parts of a body, we all have different roles to play and responsibilities to accomplish.
- No one part is capable of playing all the parts or learning how to play all the parts. Listen as the eye might, it cannot and will never hear like the ear.

Paul's arguments strengthen the conviction that the leader must not see himself or herself as the whole with subordinate helpers—the genius with a thousand helpers. The leader is himself or herself a part of the greater whole in service to God. A significant function of the leader is to manage people and their efforts so that all of the parts are aligned and playing their appropriate roles. Just as important is the realization that the body of Christ is not made of interchangeable and easily movable parts. Staff members and key volunteers have both gifts and areas where they are not gifted. They have roles for which they are capable as well as roles they are incapable of performing. The leader's task is to:

- identify, recruit, and retain the persons who have the right gifts and can fulfill the roles and responsibilities needed by the full body
- resource, support, and hold staff and volunteers accountable for their parts of the whole
- align the parts—the gifts, roles, and responsibilities—so that the body can move and the individual parts, including the leader, do not overshadow or cripple the integrity of the whole

Senior clergy and personnel committees at times are surprised to realize that a healthy concept of the body of Christ does not reflect some of our norms of congregational practice—norms that insist on a democracy of attention in which all people are expected to be given equal status and importance and every voice is to be attended to and heard equally. False assumptions of democracy and false assumptions of equal need and capacity of all staff members, in fact, reduce the effectiveness of ministry. Using the results from a large and comprehensive study based on in-depth interviews by the Gallup Organization of more than eighty thousand managers in more than four hundred companies, Buckingham and Coffman suggest that good managers, in fact, must break some strong dominant assumptions and organizational norms in order to steward and direct an organization's human resources productively. The following are four assumptions and norms that good leaders must break:

Assumptions to be broken:

- Do not believe that people can achieve anything to which they set their mind.
- Do not try to help a person overcome his or her weaknesses.
- Disregard the Golden Rule. Do not assume that everyone should be treated the same or that everyone should be treated the way that you—as the leader—prefer to be treated.
- Play favorites. The larger portion of your attention should be directed to the persons who are most productive.[6]

A leader cannot call forth skills and interests that a staff member does not have. Leaders should not invest themselves in changing people. Leaders must give serious and careful attention to what each individual staff person needs and appreciates to shape and support her or his work.

Personal and professional development of a staff member is the task of the staff member, not the leader. The leader's role is limited to being clear about the work to be done; providing—or providing access to—the needed resources; and setting the vision and challenge. The response of preparation and performance, as well as personal development for the future, belongs to the individual staff member. For the leader to assume responsibility to change the other person (even for an intended improvement) seems audacious and paternalistic—with the leader believing that he or she knows all the answers and what is best for the other person.[7]

What Do People Need from Their Work?

Over the last twenty-five years, the well-known Gallup Organization, which provides survey research results to organizations, has interviewed more than one million employees, asking hundreds of different questions on every aspect of their work. Searching for patterns in their research, Gallup identified twelve questions that best measure the strength of a workplace.[8] In other words, what do staff look for in meaningful work and a healthy place in which

to do that work? The most important questions asked by workers
are the following:

1. Do I know what is expected of me at work?
2. Do I have the materials and equipment I need to do my
    work right?
3. At work, do I have the opportunity to do what I do best
    every day?
4. In the last seven days, have I received recognition or
    praise for doing good work?
5. Does my supervisor, or someone at work, seem to care
    about me as a person?
6. Is there someone at work who encourages my develop-
    ment?
7. At work, do my opinions seem to count?
8. Does the mission/purpose of my company make me feel
    my job is important?
9. Are my coworkers committed to doing quality work?
10. Do I have a best friend at work?
11. In the last six months, has someone at work talked to me
    about my progress?
12. This last year, have I had opportunities at work to learn
    and grow?

The top six. If twelve questions are too much to keep in mind,
then pay attention to the first six. The top six questions clearly are
the most powerful drivers for staff—with links to producing performance outcomes and employee retention. (Retention also correlates
with question 7.) It is important for leaders to have some awareness
of and pay attention to the needs that staff have in their work with
the congregation.

The Human Resource Cycle

Managing and directing staff members as human resources cannot be an overly complex task for senior clergy and others who

supervise staff. Strategies for managing staff must be developed to fit into the natural flow of work and ministry. Large corporate or manufacturing organizations typically separate out responsibilities in a hierarchical fashion by identifying certain persons for leadership functions, who are to be supported by others who have management functions, while yet others are assigned to production functions. In contrast, congregations are exceedingly complex network (relational) organizations with difficult-to-define outcomes; a proportionately small number of employees; and the functions of leader, manager, and producer often compressed into the same persons. Leaders in congregations are not helped by developing complex and time-consuming practices to work with staff. Because working with and directing staff are centrally important in congregations, the ways in which senior leaders do this work must be natural and organic and must not add undue burden to already overtaxed persons, including the leader.

Having a basic road map in mind will clarify for the leader what is needed to manage people as resources for ministry. Collins and Devanna provide the following map of the generic human resource functions that need to be given attention:[9]

Figure 1.1
The Human Resource Cycle

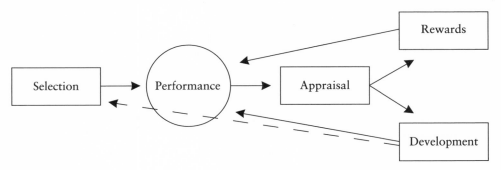

While the following chapters do not attempt full discussion or provide resources for all steps in the human resource cycle, the leader will find helpful ideas and proven tools used in congregations to apply in his or her role as staff leader.

Chapter 2

Employment and Covenant
The Nature of Working Relationships in Congregations

Pastors Mark and Cindy and Rabbi Ben are good friends and colleagues. For ten years they have ministered in neighboring communities, and over the years their ministries have flourished along with their friendship. Mark, Cindy, and Ben meet monthly to support one another in ministry and to talk about the challenges inherent in leading congregations, particularly the challenges of supervising staff teams. The three think alike on most critical issues of ministry. However, their conversation at a recent meeting focused on one aspect of congregational life where they see things quite differently.

Mark regularly develops his lay leaders into paid employees of the congregation. From Mark's perspective the employment of church members is a logical progression in the development of their giftedness. He grooms people in ministry, and when their role begins to consume more time than a volunteer can reasonably be expected to contribute, or when the ministry requires more consistent focus, he converts the role into an employment relationship. Mark can't conceive of running the church any other way. Employed members of the church make up a significant core of his team, and he finds church members to be the most highly committed, enthused team members.

Cindy's experience couldn't be any more different. When she first arrived at the church, she was saddled with a problem employee who was also a longtime church member. Agnes was the church office manager and had occupied that role for fifteen years prior to Cindy's arrival. She had been a member of the congregation for thirty-two years. Everyone in Cindy's church knew that Agnes underperformed in her role. Key leaders were also painfully aware of the damage that Agnes did in the church by gossiping and undermining the authority of the pastor. But no one seemed prepared to do anything about this problem employee. Agnes was a widow with no other visible means of support. Her skill base was poor and she was in her late fifties, making the likelihood of employment elsewhere highly unlikely. Cindy had to wait for Agnes to retire, enduring four years of church office incompetence. After that experience Cindy swore she would never again allow a church member to become a church employee. At least she could fire underperforming nonmembers!

Ben is open to the possibility of hiring a synagogue member but avoids it when he can. It just isn't a big deal to Ben either way. However, at their last meeting Ben wanted to talk about something else that has been troubling him. Ben's congregation has recently been through a board transition. He has a new board president who is a young, successful business executive. Ben likes the new president but is nervous about some of the changes the president wants to introduce. At the last board meeting the president announced his intent to implement a full-blown staff performance management system into the life of the congregation—one that parallels the system he successfully implemented in his own business two years ago. The board eagerly voted in the proposed plan. Ben isn't sure how he feels about the pending change. He is troubled by something in the pit of his stomach that tells him that systems from the world of business don't belong in synagogues. Isn't the fundamental nature of relationships in congregations and businesses different? Should they be sharing similar performance measurement systems? Ben likes the idea of more accountability in the synagogue; he just isn't sure that this is the way to go.

The subjects discussed by Mark, Cindy, and Ben often emerge when congregational leaders gather to discuss supervision practices. The questions take on a variety of forms, including:

- Is there something fundamentally different about the nature of an employment relationship in a congregation, by virtue of the fact that it is a faith-based community?

- Should we hire members as employees? If so, how do we manage the boundary between employment and membership?
- Do congregations have an inherent duty to offer greater tolerance to an underperforming staff member? Isn't firing someone tantamount to abandoning or giving up on that person?
- If we have to fire someone, should the way in which we do that look fundamentally different than it would in the workplace because we are a faith community?
- Do we have a higher sense of obligation to our employees than other employers do?
- Can I be a pastor or rabbi to someone who is also my employee?
- Should we use human resource management tools from the world of business in the world of congregations?

We suspect that with little effort you could add another five or six questions to this list. While each of these questions may appear unique, collectively this group of questions stems from one root question: *When a congregation chooses to pay someone for work done on its behalf, what is the fundamental nature of that relationship?*

Covenant: The Foundation of Congregational Life

The foundational relationship in congregational life is the covenantal relationship. A covenant is a formal agreement or treaty between two parties with each party assuming some obligation in the relationship. Covenantal relationships are characterized by mutual need, mutual promise, faithfulness, and unconditional love.

The covenant relationship between God and God's people is woven inextricably into the fabric of our faith stories. God creates a covenant with Noah, establishing Noah and his offspring as cocreators of life on earth (Gen. 9:1-17). God also enters into a covenantal relationship with Abraham, promising to deliver

descendants and land in return for Abraham's faithfulness (Genesis
15). Later Moses enters into covenantal relationship with God on
behalf of the Israelites. God assures the people, "Now if you obey
me fully and keep my covenant, then out of all nations you will be
my treasured possession." (Exod. 19:5). The lineage is continued
with David when God promises, "I will make your name great, like
the names of the greatest men of the earth. And I will provide a
place for my people Israel and will plant them so that they can have
a home of their own and no longer be disturbed" (2 Sam. 7:9-10).
In the Christian tradition Jesus is portrayed as the fulfillment of
God's covenant promise, extending the covenant beyond the Jewish
tradition to all who believe in Christ Jesus (Galatians 3).

Communities of faith founded in the Judeo-Christian tradition
are built on the core assumption that God seeks relationship with
God's people and that the nature of this relationship is covenantal.
And so we believe that our relationships with one another ought to
reflect the fundamental nature of our relationship with God, which
is characterized by mutual caring, mutual promise, faithfulness, and
unconditional love. The foundational nature of covenant makes the
institutional life of congregations unique from every other form
of institutional life. While every human institution relies on some
definition of healthy relationship, congregational relationships begin
with a high standard of relational ethics informed by this notion of
covenant.

What, then, is the nature of an employment relationship in an
organization that revolves around covenant? Does the covenantal
relationship between members of a congregation extend itself to the
congregation's employees? How might those relationships be the
same or different? To think effectively about these questions, perhaps
it would be useful to think about the fundamental similarities and
differences between covenant relationships among members of a
congregation and employment relationships outside the walls of the
congregation. After we explore the fundamental differences between
these two kinds of relationship, we can evaluate how employment
relationships ought to work inside of a congregation.

The following chart illustrates basic comparisons. The chart
reveals that in some ways the two relationships are very closely
related and in other capacities they are quite different.

Table 2.1
Covenant vs. Employment: Fundamental Similarities and Differences

	Covenantal Relationships	Employment Relationships
Underlying ethical orientation	**Cocreation:** Partners mutually engaged in creation, fulfillment, extending the kingdom of God. **Benevolence:** The entity with the greater power looks out for the best interest of those with lesser power.	**Utilitarian:** Together we pursue a course of action that will produce the most good (or pleasure over pain), for the greatest number of people.
Time frame	**Ongoing, unending**	**Temporal** Hiring (beginning), termination (ending)
Focus	**Mutual relationship,** mutual need, mutual promise, mutual call	**Supply and demand** Maximize bottom line Achieve defined outcomes
Values	**Protecting the "least of these,"** submission, the pursuit of justice, righteousness, and mercy	**Offer and Acceptance,** fairness, equity
Objective of the relationship	Fulfillment of a **promise** (beyond the letter of the law)	Fulfillment of a **contract**
Outcomes sought	**Restored community,** right relationship, blessed future	**Career satisfaction,** monetary reward, professional growth, job security, achievement
What failure looks like	**Broken relationship** Isolation Separation from God and one another	**Terminated relationship** Firing Unemployment
Accountability requires	Clearly stating expectations; honoring the covenant; **reconciliation when the covenant is broken**	Clearly stating expectations; honoring the conditions of the agreement; **mediation when the contract is broken**

Perhaps the area where covenant and employment are most different is in their underlying ethical orientation. At the core of covenantal relationships are the notions of cocreation and benevolence. Those in covenantal relationships become cocreators in ministry. We labor together as people of faith to bring the kingdom of God to fruition in whatever way we define it as a faith community. Covenantal relationships are also marked by benevolence. We seek to protect one another and others outside of the faith community from imbalances of power; those in positions of power look out for the best interest of those on the margins.

While some employment relationships may manifest these ethical proclivities, the employment relationship emerges from a different ethical orientation. The employment relationship is at its heart a utilitarian relationship. Employer and employee come together in relationship because it makes sense. The two recognize that they are better together than alone. An employment relationship makes sense when the combination of employer and employee produces the greatest balance of pleasure over pain for the greatest number of people. In other words, the relationship has to "pay off" in some meaningful way. Everyone is better off because the employer and employee work together. When the relationship no longer serves a utilitarian purpose, the relationship no longer needs to exist.

Consequently, the fundamental time orientation in covenant and employment relationships is different. Covenantal relationships are ongoing, never ending. Each of the biblical covenants requires something of the people as they seek God's protection and blessing. However, even when God is angry with people for violating the covenant, God stays in relationship. This is best illustrated by the prophetic imagery of Hosea and his wife. The prophet continually reestablishes relationship with his wife in spite of her many indiscretions. Similarly, God always welcomes back an errant people. That's the nature of covenant. Employment relationships don't have the same ongoing orientation. An employment relationship has a definitive beginning (date hired) and a definitive ending point (termination date). When the relationship is over, it is fully over; we don't seek to reestablish relationship. We don't begin employment relationships with the expectation that they will end at a particular point in time. However, most of us anticipate that at some point the employer-employee bond will no longer make sense, and either the employer or the employee will make a move to end the relationship.

Because of their utilitarian purpose, employment relationships work on the basis of supply and demand. We each have something to offer that the other needs; the balance of supply and demand defines the boundary of the relationship. I decide how much to pay you on the basis of how much in demand your skills are in the marketplace. As we work together, we pursue a focus on the bottom line, always balancing the expense of how much you cost as an employee with the level of benefit or revenue that you bring to the organization. We measure the effectiveness of the relationship according to defined and measurable outcomes. Covenantal relationships have a different focus. When we choose to be in covenant with one another, we focus on our mutual need to be together and the mutual promise that we have made to one another, regardless of how beneficial we find it in the moment. We serve one another out of a mutual sense of call to the joint mission we have engaged. The measurable success of that mission is not our concern; the strength of the relationship is.

When we come together to explore the boundaries of an employment relationship, we will talk about values such as acceptance, fairness, and equity. We measure the rightness of the relationship by determining how fairly people are being treated and how equally the work is being shared. Ultimately the objective of an employment relationship is the fulfillment of a contract (actual or implied). Within covenantal relationship we measure our success or failures by different standards—our ability to be a blessing to one another and the extent to which our relationship produces justice, mercy, and righteousness in the world. Ultimately the objective of a covenantal relationship is the fulfillment of a promise.

We can tell that covenantal relationships are working well when the community feels whole, when relationships are right or restored, and when our sense of the future feels blessed. We typically would not look to an employment relationship for the same outcomes. Employees know that the relationship is good when they experience a sense of career satisfaction, when the monetary rewards seem appropriate for the energies invested, when they perceive that they are growing in their work, and when they experience a sense of achievement.

It is generally pretty easy to recognize the brokenness that occurs when an employment relationship fails. Someone is fired, someone is unemployed, someone is being sued, and the relationship between employer and employee is permanently terminated. Likewise, it is easy to recognize the signs of a failed covenantal relationship, although the signs are different; parties to the covenant are isolated from one another, out of relationship, separated from God and one another.

For all of their differences, covenant and employment relationship share one remarkable similarity: both require the partners in the relationship to hold one another mutually accountable. Covenant and employment accountability both require three things:

1. We must be clear about our expectations of one another.
2. We must honor the conditions of the agreement we have crafted.
3. We must seek restoration when the relationship is not working well.

In employment relationships the restoration that we seek is most often in the form of mediation. We simply want to get back to a place of fair and honest mutual expectations. In covenant the restoration we seek typically requires something more. When covenant has been broken, we need to be reconciled to one another, which is a deeper form of healing that requires openness, vulnerability, and mutual understanding.

Why Is Blending Covenant and Employment So Difficult?

Now that we have explored the distinctions and similarities between covenant and employment relationships, let's examine the distinctiveness of employment relationships that occur within covenant communities. What is the fundamental nature of employment in a congregational setting? Is it possible for a congregation to genuinely embrace covenant and employment relationships at the same time? Yes. Can we have employees who are not part of the covenant? Absolutely. Can we have employees who are also members, so that we simultaneously manage employment and covenantal relationships? Many congregations do this very well. However, if we are going to balance and/or blend covenant and contract, we clearly need to understand the differences between the two, understand which we are trying to honor at any given time, and make certain that we have adequately defined the boundaries of our employment relationships so that they stay healthy. There are several fundamental reasons why congregations find it difficult to jointly manage covenant and employment relationships.

First, many members of our congregations don't know what covenantal relationships are and have rarely experienced one. Consumerism and capitalism have crept so far into the culture of the church that most members have a utilitarian approach to their involvement with the congregation. They will invest in the life of the congregation on the basis of what they receive in return. If their membership in the life of the congregation doesn't provide a surplus of benefit over and above their level of investment, they will end the relationship and go elsewhere. The only aspects of covenantal relationship they grasp are the expression of benevolence and a general attitude of caretaking. This distorted view of covenant makes it confusing for them to think about an employment relationship informed by covenant. They want employment relationships in the church to look different from employment relationships in the secular world, but they don't know how to express that. So they seek to be kinder, gentler, and more understanding. They don't want to demand accountability, and they let poor performance go unaddressed. If our members had a better understanding of covenantal relationship, they would have a better understanding of how to approach an employment relationship informed by covenant.

A second reason congregations find it difficult to jointly manage covenant and relationship is that they are not careful about establishing boundaries when they hire members. If and when those relationships go wrong, they can't figure out which set of relationship principles to apply in straightening them out. If a congregation decides to hire a member, they need to have a conversation about how the employment relationship will work within the covenantal relationship that the employee already has with the congregation. The member needs to understand how this new relationship will function within the context of the other and how the employment relationship may modify certain aspects of the covenantal relationship. The employee also needs to understand that the employment relationship may end, but the covenantal relationship will continue to stand. Let's look at an example of a covenantal relationship gone bad.

Cathy worked as a faithful children's ministry volunteer at Wellspring Church for years. She loved the children, she was a natural with them, and she particularly enjoyed her working relationship with Pastor Ray, which had grown deeper over the years. When the director of children's ministry at Wellspring resigned, it seemed logical to everyone that Cathy would be offered the position. Cathy agreed, and her first year in the position was wonderful. Ray spent lots of time with Cathy, developing her into a management team member, and then he began to pull back to provide Cathy with more autonomy and room to develop the position. That's when things began to go badly. Cathy became angry and resentful about the changing nature of her relationships in the church, about Ray's increasing emotional distance, and about the never-ending demands that long-time friends placed on her now that she was a paid staff member. Cathy discovered that when she came to church on Sunday mornings, she no longer had a meaningful worship experience because of all her work obligations. Eventually she resigned from the position and began looking for a new church home.

When it became clear to pastor Ray that Cathy was considering leaving the congregation, he called her in for a long overdue conversation about what had gone wrong. After a lengthy and painful conversation about failed dreams and broken expectations, Ray finally began to piece together where they had failed. When Cathy was a volunteer, she loved to think of herself as a favored sheep within the flock. She knew that Pastor Ray relied on her to watch after the other sheep, and she enjoyed his attention and his pastoral care. Somehow she expected that becoming an employee would bring her into an even closer relationship under the watchful eye of her pastor (the shepherd). And during the first year it had. When Ray told Cathy that he was training her to become a shepherd alongside him so that she could develop her own flock, Cathy became angry. She had never desired to serve in that capacity. She wanted to retain her status as one of the favored sheep, in special relationship with the shepherd. She wanted to have the same relationship that she'd always had with other members of the congregation. Instead, she lost her place of worship. She no longer feels that she has a pastor, and the nature of most of her friendships within the church have irreversibly changed. A careful conversation with Cathy at the time of the employment decision could have avoided much of the pain of the last year. What we learn from this example is that members who are considering becoming employees must be guided through an exploration of the differences between covenant and employment.

The final reason that congregations have such difficulty managing employment and covenant is that they ignore the accountability component inherent in both relationships. In our earlier exploration of employment and covenantal relationships, we discovered that accountability was the one area in which both types of relationships are most alike. When people fail to honor the basic needs of the other, whether the relationship is covenant or employment, they must be held accountable. Failure to seek accountability in our relationships weakens those relationships, whether they are covenant or employment in nature.

Let's reflect back upon the example of Agnes in the opening paragraphs of this chapter. Cindy's congregation didn't feel that they could hold Agnes accountable in her role as office manager because she was a longtime church member with challenging financial needs. Remember that Agnes was a gossip and frequently undermined the authority of her pastor, in addition to being a poor office manager. This means that Agnes regularly failed in both her employment relationship with the congregation and in her covenantal relationship with them. She was not held accountable for either relationship, and therefore her congregation failed her. They didn't hold up their side of either the employment or covenant relationship.

Cindy claimed that the problem with hiring members is that you can't fire them. Most congregations are so poor at holding their employees or members accountable that the problem isn't really associated with membership. It really didn't matter to Cindy's church whether Agnes was a member. After fifteen years of employment, and facing a challenging personal financial situation, Agnes probably would not have been fired even if she hadn't been a member. Firing a longtime employee is a difficult and messy task, regardless of whether the employee is a member.

What Can We Expect?

To thrive institutionally, congregations must combine covenantal and employment relationship. What can we reasonably expect of ourselves and our employees so that both types of relationships will flourish in our midst? The following paragraphs outline some of the issues that need to be addressed when blending the employment and covenant relationship. For more specific guidance on how to craft the conversations that address these issues, refer to chapter 6, "Supervision as Performance Management," and chapter 8, "Helping Staff Negotiate Their Needs."

What can we expect from employees who are not members? Those of us who are members of the congregation are bound by certain obligations, by virtue of our covenant relationship with the congregation. We are challenged to claim a sense of call and vocation with respect to our work; we are bound together as co-creators striving to give birth to the kingdom of God in this world. We cannot lay those same expectations on our employees, who are not bound together with us in covenant. But we can expect certain things from our employees. We can expect that they will honor the stated values of the organization and focus their work on the strategic priorities of the congregation (as those priorities relate to their work). We can expect that our employees will not work at cross-purposes to the congregation's articulated sense of purpose.

We can expect that our employees will honor the basic provisions of their employment agreement with us and that they will accept the consequences (be held accountable) for failure to fulfill their employment obligations.

What can we expect from members who happen to be employees? Members should not receive any unfair employment advantage by virtue of the fact that they are members. Neither should they be disadvantaged as employees because of their membership status. As members of the church, they are bound by their covenantal relationship. This puts some additional burden on the employee who is a member and must own the values and purposes of the congregation at a much deeper level than the nonmember employee. However, let's be careful to draw a distinction about the need for deeper ownership of value and purpose and being abused by the congregation. Sometimes, because of their membership status, member employees are expected to be at the beck and call of every lay member of the congregation. If we need toilet paper in the bathrooms on Sunday mornings, it is the member employee who is expected to track it down and get it installed. Member employees are not owned by the congregation any more than nonmember employees are.

We must also host important conversations with member employees about their access to and use of resources, as well as their access to and use of information. Stacy is the bookkeeper at All Souls Church, as well as a member of the congregation. Stacy needs to understand that her role as bookkeeper provides her with access to member giving records and that these records are confidential. Other members of the congregation don't have access to this kind of information, and Stacy must not share this information with other members. That confidentiality agreement holds even if Stacy resigns from her employment role but maintains her membership in the congregation. In this regard, Stacy's employment status requires a higher degree of accountability than her covenantal relationship with the congregation.

Stacy and her pastor also need to have forthright discussions about how her employment time is used within the congregation. If Stacy is involved as a lay leader in roles that are outside the scope of her employment relationship, Stacy and her pastor need to monitor those roles separately. She cannot credit the time that she spends preparing to teach the third grade Sunday school class or the time she spends singing in the choir as part of her employment contract and hours. When she and the pastor talk about her role as Sunday school teacher or choir member, they both need to be cognizant of the fact that they are talking about her covenantal relationship with the congregation and not her employment relationship.

What can we expect of ourselves as employers? We must be prepared to honor the utilitarian purposes of the employment relationship. We need to hire and supervise our employees, ensuring that they are treated honestly and fairly. We must pay our workers an honest wage for the services they provide us. We must be clear about our expectations of the relationship, and we must provide regular feedback to our employees about how well or how poorly they are satisfying those expectations. We must hold our employees accountable for their performance, and we must be willing to be held accountable as employers. If we must terminate the relationship, we are bound to do so with fairness and integrity and in accordance with the laws of our state.

What additional obligation do we bear to members that happen to be employees? We must fully honor the utilitarian nature of the employment relationship we have with member employees. Because of our covenant relationship, we are also bound with these employees in an ongoing relationship that exceeds the boundaries of their employment with us. We are obligated to make certain that there are clear expectations about how both of these relationships will be honored in tandem. We should never take a member's decision to become an employee lightly. We must make certain to fully explore the boundaries of the emerging relationship by discussing the following issues:

- How their relationship with the pastor may/will change. Some pastors feel adamant that they cannot serve in a pastoral capacity to their staff members. Others feel that they can continue to be pastor in some capacity but not in others. The new employee must understand that at times the pastor will have to choose to be supervisor first and pastor secondarily or not at all.

- How their relationships with fellow members must change by virtue of their new leadership position (including confidentiality issues and new relationship boundaries). Sometimes they will need to hold other members that they have been close to at arm's distance, and at other times, members that they have been close to in the past will hold them at arm's distance because they are now an employee.
- What is likely to happen with their participation in worship? Most members who are also employees report that worship is no longer meaningful for them, either because of their many obligations in and around worship or because their involvement in planning worship takes away their sense of awe about worship. Some will find worship more meaningful for the very same reasons.
- What the expectations are regarding access to and use of resources, access to and use of information, use of employment time, access and use of the senior pastor's time, the nature of the relationship with the pastor, access to and use of money and church property.
- When and if the employment relationship ends the member's covenantal relationship will continue. We must not be naive about this kind of transition. In some instances the challenges that surround an employment termination will negatively impact the covenantal relationship in very difficult ways. A member who has become an employee can almost never step back into the same kind of relationship he or she had before becoming an employee.

What can we say to those who want to use business practices to manage our employment relationships? When congregational leaders push for the introduction of business tools, they are generally looking for greater performance accountability in the congregation. They understand the utilitarian nature of business employment relationships, and so, without reference to any other type of relationship, this is what they push for in the church. We need to teach the language of covenant so that our leaders understand the fundamental differences and so that we can explore ways to introduce accountability in such a way that both covenant and employment relationships are honored. We need to honor and affirm their desire for greater accountability, which is a significant feature in both employment and covenant relationships.

The world of business makes use of some performance management systems that are outright awful, that don't honor the basic ethical requirements of a healthy utilitarian employment relationship, let alone a covenantal relationship. On the other hand, there are many excellent performance management tools used within the world of business that could be adapted effectively for use in congregational settings. With this book we attempt to do some of that work for you, by providing basic frameworks and approaches to thinking about employment relationships in congregational settings. However, if business leaders in your congregation bring forward a specific performance management system that they would like to use in your congregation, use the following five questions to evaluate the fit of that system in a covenantal setting:

1. Will this system honor the basic utilitarian nature of an employment relationship and encourage/support the benevolent and cocreator aspects of covenantal relationship?
2. Do the various components of this performance measurement system protect the rights and needs of the "least of these" within our community and beyond?
3. Will this system allow for the movement of God's Spirit and the discernment of God's will in our midst?
4. Does this system of managing our employees promote shared power and the charitable use of power?
5. Will these tools build accountability into our system—the kind of accountability that encourages redemption, reconciliation, and restored relationships?

Covenant relationships and employment relationships possess remarkably different features, but they are not mutually exclusive.

The head of staff who is cognizant of the differences and carefully articulates the boundaries for employees and congregants will be successful in creating a healthy staff team environment.

Chapter 3

The Importance of Outcomes

An old saying goes "If you don't know where you are going, any path will get you there." This suggests that if you are not clear about what you, your staff, and your congregation are to "produce" in ministry, what the clear outcomes of your work are to be, then it is okay for staff members to spend their time on whatever their current practices or preferences of work might be. This leads to assumptions that work—any work—is appropriate whether it is making a needed difference or not.

The dilemma is that typically when staff do not know what they are to produce, or when staff do not know what they are being held accountable to produce, they tend to value and measure their work by the amount of time consumed or the number of tasks accomplished. We all have been in supervision meetings with staff or evaluation meetings with personnel committees where a person's work was measured by how many hours was spent doing the work or how many visits, phone calls, reports, dollars, or volunteers were involved. The number of hours, visits, calls, reports, and so on is not a measure of what is *produced* in ministry but rather a measure of what is *expended* in ministry. Without a clear and shared outcome in place for a staff person's work, it is impossible to judge if the expenditure of hours, activities, and resources was appropriate or effective. The real issue of hours and resources is not whether they were spent but whether they moved the congregation toward the outcome of ministry to which it is called by its mission. Staff members are not paid to work hard, but to achieve ministry.

Even more debilitating than simply working hard along any path because you don't know where you are going is the truism of all living systems: *When a system doesn't know what to do, it does what it knows.* It is widely recognized that ministry is in a time of great transition because we are learning how to do ministry in a culture that has greatly changed. In what often is described as an in-between time, leaders have recognized that what many congregations know how to do no longer works well, but many congregations do not yet know what will work or are not yet practiced at doing what they have discovered will work. When a system does not know what to do, it does what it knows. The consequence is that when outcomes are unclear, staff members are tempted to spend increasing amounts of time doing what they know how to do by attending committee meetings, revising structure, and working harder and longer at programs that used to work—with the hope that the extra effort at known tasks will make the difference.

Most Congregations Don't Know What They "Produce"

Leaders of congregations are more likely to have a good idea of what they "do" (the activities of the congregation) than of what those activities are to "produce." Keeping people in the congregation happy so that they don't complain is not an appropriate product of ministry. More people participating in what we are doing is not necessarily a product of ministry. Yet it is hard for leaders to get more specific about what is to be produced in ministry, such as introducing a new generation to the faith, deepening the life of individuals so that their faith makes a practical difference in their daily living, or building a "bridge" into the community and the larger world that will introduce new people to faith.

For mainline, established congregations—Protestant, Catholic, and Jewish—the question of product is new and did not need to be answered in the past. In an earlier time, these three dominant expressions of faith in the American experience had an assigned cultural role to play in the sociological structure of our nation. It was sufficient simply to be a "type" of congregation—Protestant, Catholic, or Jewish. That identity provided adequate explanation of what the congregation was to do. It may be helpful to view a very similar experience through the recent history of the South African Dutch Reformed Church, which had a large and significant cultural role to undergird and preserve apartheid. In many people's experience, the "reason" for the Dutch Reformed congregation in the history of South Africa was intimately tied to supporting the dominant culture. With such a strong cultural reason to "be," congregations did not need to know what they were to produce; they simply needed to exist. Since the fall of apartheid, leaders of the Dutch Reformed Church are finding it necessary to struggle to help congregations envision and become clear about what they are to do and what they are to produce now that the cultural reason of apartheid no longer holds sway. Never having to ask the question of purpose or outcomes in the past makes current wrestling with purpose exceedingly difficult. The situation for established American congregations is similar now that the cultural reason of providing a place for membership and national identity is no longer the dominant reason for the congregation to exist.

Outcomes Describe What It Will Be Like in One to Three Years If the Staff and Congregation Are Faithful to Their Mission and Call

Mission statements are critically important. When well developed, they are statements of identity, purpose, and context, answering the following formation questions:

- Who are we?
- What has God called us to be and do?
- Who is our neighbor?[1]

Despite their importance, mission statements commonly are too general and attempt to speak for too long of a time period, which prevents them from providing clear and immediate direction for ministry. It is difficult to structure ministry without a mission statement. A general mission statement, however, is insufficient to develop clear strategies and make decisions about aligning resources to pursue those strategies.

Outcomes provide the critical next level of specificity of calling and commitment that the congregation needs to understand clearly. Outcomes can be used to do the following:

- develop strategies
- set goals with staff
- answer questions about needed resources
- develop timelines
- provide structures of accountability
- give clarity to goals, making it possible to explain to the various voices in the congregation why some efforts have been given priority attention

Outcomes Need to Be Clear and Concise

What is to be different in this congregation, in the community, and in the lives of individuals in the next one to three years because of our call to ministry? Outcomes need to be specific by stating clear differences within a specified amount of time. Outcomes go a step beyond saying what we will work on and actually *describe what will be different* if we are faithful in working on our call to ministry.

Outcomes Need to Be Firm in Purpose but Flexible in Strategy

In a fast-changing environment, it is possible to identify what we are to produce, but it is much more difficult to know from the outset what it will take to accomplish the outcome. Ends can be identified. Directions can be set. But strategies often need to be learned along the way. Leadership in the contemporary congregation, in fact, involves learning how to do ministry while actually doing it in a fluid and changing time. To be effective, the description of the outcome needs to be firm and in place. The way we get to the outcome needs to be held loosely and be malleable to allow new learnings that we will uncover as we do the work. The idea of being *firm in purpose but flexible in strategy* is a basic principle of the organization of behavior for all vital living systems.[2]

The tension between being both firm and flexible can be seen in the long history of Mission San Luis Rey, which was founded in 1798 as the eighteenth in the chain of twenty-one California missions on the Camino Real as a part of the Spanish conquest of that new region. Throughout its long history, the purpose of the mission always has remained the same: to make God known. The strategies for this unchanging central purpose, however, have had to change over the years. Initially the strategy was to make God known by converting Native Americans to Christianity. Historically and morally this strategy became inappropriate, yet the purpose of the mission remained the same. By late in the nineteenth century, the mission was redeveloped as a Franciscan missionary college, providing a seminary to train priests for ordination in order to make God known—the same purpose but a new strategy based on what was learned over the years about ministry in the new land. During the more recent period of the twentieth century, the number of persons studying for the priesthood and the number of seminaries needed in the United States fell sharply so that the strategy of being a seminary could no longer be maintained. The response of Mission San Luis Rey was to transform itself into a retreat center for Christian formation, which is the role that the mission plays today within the Roman Catholic and larger Christian community. Its purpose to make God known stood firm and unchanged, but the mission had to shift its strategy again because of what it was learning and experiencing in the environment in which it lives.[3]

Congregations in the present cultural reality of quick change do not need centuries of history to experience the same need for being firm in purpose but flexible in strategy. Being clear and firm about purpose is now even more critical. Such firmness needs to be partnered with strategies for addressing the purpose that have a high level of flexibility and adaptability that will respond to what is changing and being learned along the way.

Outcomes Need to Be "Visible"—They Need to Help People "See" What Is to Be Produced

The classic difference between a mission statement and a vision statement is that the mission statement describes what is to be done while the vision statement draws a verbal picture of what the results will look like if the mission is accomplished. The verbal picture is necessary to help people have a perceptual idea of the target: what will it look like? As noted, it is difficult if not impossible to be able to state from the outset what will happen and what will work in ministry in a fast-changing environment. Creativity, invention, and adaptation will be needed along the way. It, therefore, is inappropriate to hold leaders and staff accountable for an expected outcome if the shape of that outcome needs to change while the work is being done. The verbal picture of the outcome nevertheless provides the direction: "This is what we are after." Without the picture it is difficult for leaders and staff to know how to shape their work. The final results may—and probably will—vary from the original picture. Nonetheless, there needs to be a visual map from the beginning that will set direction.

You Don't Need to Know How to Get There to Name the Destination

We started with "If you don't know where you are going, any path will get you there." Here we are working with a much more important corollary: "Knowing where you are going is much more important than knowing how you will get there." Times of great change are moments of invention. New things need to be tried. Experiments need to be mounted. We need to be guided by what we are learning more than by what we already know.

Claiming a clear outcome for ministry can be an anxious moment for the senior clergy and the board of a congregation because of our limited assumptions about leadership that insist that if we name the goal, we need to know how to get there. Senior clergy struggle with supervising staff in new work because they feel the inappropriate burden of needing to tell staff what to do when they are aware they are not themselves certain.

Indeed, this book, which includes supervision resources, is a product of the need for leaders to supervise others in work that is being learned and invented along the way. There will be recurring invitations and admonitions all along the way for the senior clergy and the governing board to release the need to direct and control work that cannot easily be foreseen and foretold. Supervision will

be approached as a task of providing structured conversations, resources, and accountability that will make it possible for staff and
leaders to work toward outcomes. In fact, in the current environment, the leader who believes that he or she needs to know not only
what is to be done but how to do it is a barrier to ministry. Great
change takes place in the wilderness of new times. When Moses tried
to do all the leadership tasks by himself, he became exhausted and
the work of the people suffered greatly. It was when he was able to
draw the picture of the Promised Land and work with Aaron and
others to figure out the trip, day by day, that the slaves transformed
themselves into the nation of Israel.

The Role of the Senior Clergy

The role of the senior clergy in a congregation is to live in the middle
and bring shape to the ministry. That role involves the following:

- working with the governing board and key leaders to discern
  the future of the congregation, to keep leaders spiritually
  grounded, and to shape the mission for the future
- working with the staff and the governing board to develop
  the appropriate outcomes—the differences needed in one to
  three years—so that the mission takes shape and direction
- supervising staff and key leaders to shape and pursue the
  implementation of the outcomes in faithful ways

It is important for senior clergy to understand the role they play
between the board and the staff.

- The board sets the mission and the direction for the ministry
  of the congregation. It is not helpful—indeed it is harmful—
  for the board to involve itself in the ongoing management
  of the church and its outcomes. This is particularly true the
  larger the congregation.
- The staff operates on a management level, developing ways
  in which the outcomes can be addressed. While their work
  and training give them insight and information on the larger

ministry of the congregation, their point of accountability
is to that part of the work that the board has given them
to do.

It is the senior clergy who live between these two parts of the
"body" of the congregation—to keep them connected and to be sure
each is doing the appropriate work. Supervision is a key tool.

Clear Outcomes Are the Primary Tool for Effective Staff Supervision

An Example

What follows is an example of a congregation's mission/vision
statement and the subsequent outcomes, which describe what is to
be different in one and three years because of the congregation's
mission.

- *Size.* This document comes from a congregation with 2,100
  members and an average worship attendance of 850 people.
  The senior minister has as his direct reports (the persons
  he personally supervises) three other clergy and one lay
  executive staff member. There are a number of other full-
  and part-time program and support staff who are supervised
  by others.
- *The larger mission/vision.* When reading the following
  example of outcomes, it will be helpful to keep in mind
  the congregation's mission/vision statement, out of which
  the outcomes grew. Note the general nature of the mission/
  vision statement and how difficult it would be to direct and
  supervise the work without clearer outcomes through which
  expectations can be defined.
- *Adaptability.* Outcomes need to be unique and specific to
  the congregation where they are formed. In style, content,
  and complexity, the outcomes must match the specific
  congregation for which they are developed. The following
  is offered as a good example, not as a template.

Acme Congregational Church
Anytown, Anystate
January 1, 2008

Our Mission/Vision

The Vision
*Acme Congregational Church of Anytown: On the move to make
a difference through Jesus Christ.*

We are a family of believers being transformed by the power of
God's love through Jesus Christ. We are on the move through
intentional ministry that makes a difference in the world, which
needs to experience that same transformation.

We fulfill this vision through:

- providing meaningful, inspiring worship
- studying God's Word individually and in small groups
- integrating prayer into our daily lives
- empowering individuals to discover and use their spiritual
  gifts
- offering ministries of outreach to our community and
  world
- extending compassionate care to those in need
- welcoming new ideas and methods of doing ministry
  inspired by the movement of God's Spirit

Our Statement of Outcomes

What needs to be in place and what needs to be different in order
for us to be faithful to our vision?

Providing meaningful, inspiring worship

One-Year Outcomes:

- Put forth more intentional effort in striving toward excellence in worship leadership.
- Develop creative worship planning team for traditional worship.
- Consider committing to thematic consistency in all worship services on any given Sunday morning.

Three-Year Outcomes:

- Implement a new weekly worship service at a time other than Sunday morning (perhaps Celebrate Recovery).
- Have in place a fully functioning creative worship team for each approach to worship.

Studying God's Word individually and in small groups

One-Year Outcomes:

- Establish a systematic approach to challenging the congregation with individual Bible reading/study.
- Continue intentional development of small group study opportunities.
- Have all full-time clergy teach at least one class in fall and spring.
- Establish accountability for personal study among senior leadership team.

Three-Year Outcomes:

- Implement a fully developed intentional approach to individual congregational study that is engaged in by at least five hundred people in the congregation.

- Have a diverse small group ministry in place that involves at least four hundred people.

Integrating prayer into our daily lives

One-Year Outcomes:

- Develop intentional focus on lifting up prayer as one of the keys to our vision statement.
- Continue the senior pastor's prayer rotation through the congregation.
- Establish accountability for personal prayer among senior leadership team.

Three-Year Outcomes:

Empowering individuals to discover and use their spiritual gifts

One-Year Outcomes:

- Develop a systematic approach to our spiritual gifts process as it relates to current members.
- Link the new member process with the spiritual gifts process.
- Develop a specific system to assist individuals who have been through the spiritual gifts class in identifying their gifts and plugging into ministry that utilizes their passion and spiritual gifts.
- Develop intentional ways to give increased visibility to the spiritual gifts focus.

Three-Year Outcomes:

- At least three hundred individuals will have completed the spiritual gifts process and will be serving in ministry according to their passion and spiritual gifts.

Offering ministries of outreach to our community and world

One-Year Outcomes:

- Develop ministries through use of the new building that will bring people from the community into our facility.
- Become intentional about increasing our twelve-step ministry outreach.
- Explore ways that our children's and youth ministry can focus more on outreach into the community.
- Move ahead with an intentional approach to the Natural Church Development process in addressing our "Minimum Factor"—need-oriented evangelism.
- Continue to clarify the role of the parish nurse in this regard.
- Schedule and complete another In His Service Day.

Three-Year Outcomes:

- Have in place a fully functioning recreation ministry for children and youth that makes regular use of our new facility. This ministry is to involve children and youth from the community.
- Establish In His Service Day as an event that occurs at least twice a year.

Extending compassionate care to those in need

One-Year Outcomes:

- Schedule at least one adult mission trip.
- Complete Habitat for Humanity house.
- Continue to add to volunteer involvement with IHN.
- Continue to explore and make a decision in regard to providing space for the Christian Service Center's ministry.

- Explore and make a decision in regard to offering day care for adults.
- Continue to expand Stephen Ministry.
- Continue to expand the role of laity in congregational care.
- Continue to clarify the role of the parish nurse in this regard.

Three-Year Outcomes:

- Schedule at least two adult mission trips annually.
- Complete another Habitat for Humanity house, with the goal of completing one house every two to three years.

Welcoming new ideas and methods of doing ministry inspired by the movement of God's Spirit

Other thoughts on what needs to be different:

- Emphasize accountability, first among the senior leadership team in regard to the spiritual disciplines of prayer, study, and stewardship of time and resources.
- Establish an intentional process by which we share information. We need an agreement among us not to hold information as a way of maintaining power and control.

PART 2
An Overview of the Performance Management Cycle

Chapter 4

The Critical Job Description

J. R. R. Tolkien's Lord of the Rings trilogy introduces Frodo Baggins, a hobbit who has been selected to serve in a very special role. Frodo has been chosen to carry a magical and powerful ring on a journey to Mount Doom, where the ring must be destroyed before evil takes possession of it. A band of devoted and talented travelers attend to Frodo along the way, but in the end it is Frodo and his loyal sidekick, Sam, who must accomplish the task.

As a character, Frodo is not particularly remarkable. He is not especially magical compared to many of the other creatures encountered in the trilogy. He is not even particularly intelligent, loyal, or courageous. Yet Frodo succeeds at the task laid before him, with some significant help along the way.

Tolkien's story illustrates several dynamics that characterize the successful management of a role. Frodo is assigned a mission that has pinpoint clarity and precision: travel to Mordor and drop the ring into the fires of Mount Doom before evil takes possession of the ring. The purpose of his role is clear, simple, and compelling.

Additionally, Frodo is clear about the essential functions required of him in his role as keeper of the ring. Carry the ring, but do not put it on your finger. Resist the temptation of power that the ring holds. Prevent the ring from returning to its original master, even though the ring desires to do so. Yield to the guidance, leadership, and protection of the fellowship, but do not let weakness in the fellowship prevent you from accomplishing your task. If necessary, travel alone to fulfill your role.

The council that appoints Frodo to this role is clear about his suitability for the task at hand. A variety of others—each cleverer and more powerful and physically able than Frodo—might have been selected for the task. Frodo was chosen because of several unique attributes that perfectly suited him for his role as ring bearer. Frodo was humble, and his humility would protect him from the incredible power of the ring. Frodo was small and unassuming; he could travel without attracting great attention. Frodo was committed to the greater good and was willing to sacrifice his very self to see the ring destroyed.

One might say that a combination of conditions allowed Frodo to fulfill his calling successfully. The role was defined for him with great clarity; the broad steps for completing the task were outlined for him; and he possessed the required attributes to complete the job. He also was supported and encouraged by critical mentors along the way. This simple combination of clarity of purpose, clarity of function, clarity of required attributes, and an abundance of support explains Frodo's accomplished journey. This combination can be used to explain success on any journey—especially the journey of ministry in a congregational setting.

Role Confusion

The concept of role is very important to the understanding of organizational behavior and success. Certain activities are expected of every staff position and of many of the volunteer positions within a congregation. Role refers to the expected behavior patterns attributed to a particular position of ministry. A role typically includes a desired set of behaviors, but it often includes a desired set of attitudes and values, as well. Sometimes the roles in a congregation are set forth explicitly. At other times, roles are clearly understood but not explicitly stated. In many instances, the role is neither clearly understood nor explicitly stated, and we have role confusion. It is this last set of circumstances that is most problematic to successful performance in ministry.

In any organizational setting a variety of factors contribute to role confusion and a resulting lack of performance. These include confusion in role perception, multiple roles, and role conflict.[1]

Confusion in *role perception* occurs when different individuals or groups have differing perceptions of the behavior that ought to be associated with a given role. Parents and their own children may not agree about what the youth pastor ought to do and how she ought to do it. The rest of the staff may have an additional set of impressions about how the youth pastor ought to represent herself as a member of the staff team. The head of staff may have yet another set of perceptions. Finally, the youth pastor herself makes certain assumptions about what she brings to the role. Conflicting role perceptions lead to conditions of uncertainty and stress for the staff member and the congregation.

Most leaders play *multiple roles* simultaneously. They occupy many different positions in a variety of organizations—home, work, school, church, and civic and professional groups. Each one of these positions requires different relationships, and these role relationships often make conflicting demands upon us. A person may be head of staff in his or her congregation. It also is likely that he or she has defined roles within a family system as spouse, parent, child, or sibling. Perhaps he or she also serves an important function somewhere in the life of your denomination. As head of staff, he or she may be expected to maintain one or more roles of leadership in the community. The combined set of expectations from serving in multiple roles can be maddening. And the behaviors required to serve simultaneously in each of those roles can produce high levels of stress.

Because of the multiplicity of roles and role sets that leaders occupy, it is possible for an individual to face a situation where there is simultaneous occurrence of two or more role requirements and the performance of one precludes the performance of the others. When this occurs, the individual faces a situation known as *role conflict*. One type of role conflict occurs when two simultaneous roles call upon value systems that violate one another or violate a basic personal value. For example, as head of staff a senior pastor may hold strong values about doing ministry through covenantal relationships with staff members. The governing board, however, may insist upon approaching the senior pastor and the members of staff as employees. When serving in the role as board member, the senior pastor is asked to operate from a set of values that contradicts the values used in the daily management of staff. This produces role conflict.[2]

What happens when the senior clergy or staff members experience too much role ambiguity or role conflict? They get stressed, and that stress manifests itself in a variety of ways, including mental and physical illness, diminished feelings of job satisfaction, and withdrawal and isolation.

The easiest and most straightforward technique for avoiding and diminishing role conflict is through dialogue and discussion about role expectations. To the extent that leaders can get clarity of purpose, function, and required competency, the effects of role ambiguity and confusion can be minimized. The job description is a straightforward tool to provide guidance in our dialogue about role clarity.

Most congregations today are clear about the need to formulate job descriptions for the all-important task of hiring new employees. We know that documentation of performance expectations is required to get the right person on our team. Many job descriptions, however, are put aside or ignored once the hiring process is complete, as if they have fulfilled all useful purpose. Nothing could be further from the truth. The job description serves many important ongoing functions in a supervisory relationship:

- as a definition of the functions, responsibilities, and core competencies of a job
- as an outline of the covenantal relationship between partners in mutual ministry
- as a mechanism for getting the right person into the right ministry position
- for performance evaluation—measuring actual performance against the standards established in the job description
- for staff member development—by clarifying, communicating, and training on updated performance standards

- for establishing legal defensibility during the hiring and termination process
- to benchmark positions for the fair and equitable assignment of salary ranges and increases
- to provide continuity in the role when people change positions—either the employee or management transitions
- to establish meaningful boundaries between roles (i.e., where does my job end and yours begin?)

Components of the Job Description

The apostle Paul's first epistle to Timothy reads like a ministry job description. At the opening of the epistle and again at its close, we find a *job summary* for Timothy that we can paraphrase like this: "Remain in Ephesus so that you may instruct people in the right doctrine. The aim of your instruction is the love that comes from a pure heart, a good conscience, and sincere faith. Guard what has been entrusted to you."

Much of the epistle is a listing of the *essential functions and requirements* for Timothy's leadership in the faith community. A few examples from the fourth chapter include:

- Have nothing to do with profane myths.
- Train yourself in godliness.
- Set your hope on the living God.
- Set the believers an example in speech and conduct, in love, in faith, and in purity.

Chapter 3 of the letter provides a listing of the *core competencies* for the roles of bishop and deacon. It offers examples of knowledge, skills, behaviors, and attitudes required to fulfill the role:

Now a bishop must be above reproach, married only once, temperate, sensible, respectable, hospitable, an apt teacher, not a drunkard, not violent but gentle, not quarrelsome, and not a lover of money. He must manage his own household well, keeping his children submissive and respectful in every way—for if someone does not know how to manage his own household, how can he take care of God's church? He must not be a recent convert, or he may be puffed up with conceit and fall into the condemnation of the devil. Moreover, he must be well thought of by outsiders, so that he may not fall into disgrace and the snare of the devil. (1 Tim. 3:2-7)

This epistle provides the same elements of clarity as outlined in the opening example of the Lord of the Rings: clarity of purpose, function, and required attributes. This provides a decent outline for the attributes of an effective job description. The author of this letter, however, did not live in the litigious environment that congregations face today. Leaders have to make certain that our job descriptions comply with the complexities of the culture's legal system.

A wide array of job description formats exist, any number of which may be appropriate for the congregational setting. An amazing variety of ministry job descriptions can be sampled by visiting www.churchstaffing.com. Not everything available at this site is good, acceptable, and/or legal. Generally speaking, a legally acceptable format, which also provides what is needed for later performance evaluation, will include the following elements, which can be seen in the sample job description included at the end of this chapter:

- the job or ministry title
- the job's Fair Labor Standards Act (FLSA) status. Is the position exempt (salaried) or nonexempt (hourly)?
- the status of the job: full-time, part-time, or temporary
- the reporting relationship
- a job summary—an overview of the job responsibilities
- essential functions of the job—the core duties that define the job, as differentiated from other duties or responsibilities
- qualifications—minimum previous experience or credentials required to do the job
- physical requirements and working conditions
- core competencies—knowledge, skills, behaviors, and results expected in the performance of this job

- the date the job description becomes effective, which will change upon any later revisions

Bear in Mind the Legalities

The term *essential functions* in job descriptions came into being in 1990 as the result of the Americans with Disabilities Act (ADA). The ADA is a federal antidiscrimination law written to protect the rights of qualified workers who are disabled. It assists qualified disabled workers in obtaining employment if they are able to perform the essential functions of a position, with or without accommodation. The ADA applies to employers who have fifteen or more employees and is enforced by the Equal Employment Opportunity Commission (EEOC).

To be essential, a duty must be inherent to the position. In other words, the job would not be the same job without that particular duty. For example, playing a musical instrument and/or conducting a musical group could arguably be included as an essential duty in a worship leader's job description. A similar skill set might be appreciated in a youth pastor, but it is probably not arguable as an essential duty of being a youth pastor. The ADA requires that you make a distinction between essential functions and "other" duties and responsibilities.

The following three markers, defined by the ADA, will help you determine whether you are working with an essential function of the job:

- The position exists to perform the function.
- There are a limited number of other employees available to perform the functions or among whom the function can be distributed.
- A function is highly specialized, and the person in the position is hired for special expertise to perform it.

The ADA also makes the listing of physical requirements an important component of a job description. Some jobs might easily be done from a sitting position; thus a person in a wheelchair would be able to do the job if otherwise qualified. But if the position requires a substantial amount of standing, walking, or stair climbing (such as a maintenance position), that should be stated in the job description. Any requirements—including the ability to speak, see, and hear—should be clearly spelled out.[3]

Also bear in mind that *reasonable accommodation* is required if a qualified worker is able to do the essential tasks of a job, especially if it would require only minor modifications. Consider this example: A senior pastor is seeking to hire someone in her office who can reproduce the weekly bulletin and monthly newsletter. She is hoping to hire someone who also could answer the phones as a backup to the church secretary. Phone answering was intended to represent less than 10 percent of the job responsibilities. One of the candidates is absolutely qualified to perform the essential functions of the job, but he is legally deaf and would not be able to answer the telephones. The reasonable accommodation requirement encourages the employer to find another way to provide phone backup for the secretary so that this otherwise qualified candidate could be employed.

Defining the Functions and Responsibilities

Leaders will find it helpful to begin by brainstorming all of the many tasks an individual may have to execute to perform the role. Then they should group the many tasks into main responsibility areas and describe those areas. The final list should include eight to twelve essential functions and other responsibilities for a full-time position. Any fewer than that and the position is probably too general to provide much accountability. Any more than that and the job description will begin to look like a job manual instead of a job description. An entry-level position will require fewer essential functions, and a senior or executive position will generally require more. When assembled, the final description should list the requirements and functions in descending order of importance.

The following selection of functions and responsibilities may help develop a starting draft of a job description. In each instance begin with a verb choice, followed by a descriptor of whom or what is being acted upon. For example:

- Provides administrative and clerical support to members of the professional staff.
- Participates in all staff meetings.
- Maintains the congregational data base.

Table 4.1

Plans and organizes	Strengthens	Serves
Manages	Directs	Repairs
Supervises	Communicates	Shepherds
Evaluates	Implements	Maintains
Coordinates	Processes	Diagnoses
Resources	Advises	Controls
Deepens	Schedules	Trains
Nurtures	Provides	Assists
Initiates	Assists	Designs
Problem solves	Equips	Guides
Participates	Leads	

Defining the Core Competencies

The "function and requirements" section discussed above answers the content or "what" questions about the job: what will the staff member be doing to fulfill this role? The core competencies section of the job description defines the knowledge, skills, behaviors, and results that are expected in the role. Core competencies seek to address the "how" and "why" questions: how will the staff member be expected to behave in this role, and why is that important?

Core competencies are critical for establishing shared standards of behavior among staff members. The core competency section of the job description will become a critical component of the performance evaluation process. Defining expectations about performance standards up front will create a better environment for discussing performance later on.

Each core competency defined should contain two critical elements:

The Behavior		**The Standard**
observable and measurable action	**+**	quantity, quality, and timeliness

Core Competency Examples[4]

- *Compassion.* Genuinely cares about people; is concerned about their work and nonwork problems; is available and ready to help; is sympathetic to the plight of others not as fortunate; demonstrates real empathy with the joys and pains of others.
- *Conflict management.* Steps up to conflicts, seeing them as opportunities; reads situations quickly; good at focused listening; can hammer out tough agreements and settle disputes equitably; can find common ground and get cooperation with minimal disruption.
- *Delegation.* Clearly and comfortably delegates both routine and important tasks and decisions; broadly shares both responsibility and accountability; trusts people to perform; lets those who report directly finish their own work.
- *Motivating others.* Creates a climate in which people want to do their best; can motivate many different individuals and groups; empowers others; shares ownership and visibility; makes each participant feel valued.

Again, it is important to limit how many core competencies you include within a job description. The eight-to-twelve range suggested for functions and requirements also applies to the core competency section. Fewer competencies will not provide a description that is comprehensive enough to frame expectations. More competencies may frustrate the staff member by overwhelming him or her with too many standards to monitor.

Participation Is Key

The key to developing good job descriptions is to solicit broad involvement from those in the congregation who ought to have a voice. Begin by identifying all of the stakeholders. These should include any employee(s) currently in the position, the manager of the employee, and any subordinates who report to the employee. Additionally, you will want to include input from members of your staff relationship committee (or its equivalent in your context). Interview a broad selection of people as you define requirements, functions, and core competencies for the position. Draft a copy of the job description and validate that draft with all of those who had input into the process.

Job descriptions are not static documents. They evolve as people bring new dimensions and increased levels of responsibility to their positions. Accordingly, job descriptions must be updated on a regular basis. Make certain that the job descriptions are updated each time a performance evaluation is delivered so that the two documents are always in agreement with one another.

Sample Job Description

Director of Small-Group Ministry

Reports to:	Pastor of Discipleship
Effective:	9/01/07
Directly supervises:	Small-groups administrator
Status:	Full-time
FLSA:	Exempt

Job Summary

The director of small-group ministry will provide dynamic leadership and oversight to the small-group ministry at ABC Congregation, equipping the process of discipleship in small-group settings.

Essential Functions

- Create and communicate a vision for small-group ministries.
- Develop a network of spiritually gifted coaches, leaders, mentors, and apprentices who can disciple people toward spiritual maturity in small-group settings.
- Promote the development and growth of a diversity of small groups, helping groups effectively launch, grow, and multiply.
- Develop and maintain a resource library of curriculum for small groups.
- Coordinate and facilitate small-group leader training events.
- Design and promote creative small-group celebrations.
- Maintain a database and Web site for small groups at ABC Congregation.
- Develop a program for evaluating the performance of small-group leaders and the functioning of their groups.

Other Responsibilities

- Participate in management team staff meetings and small-group leader staff meetings.
- Join the ABC preaching team when invited to do so by the senior pastor.
- Network in the community and with other congregations to develop and share a mutual resource base of small-group expertise.

Minimum Qualifications

- Bachelor's degree in education or religious studies (or equivalent).
- Three years' ministry experience in a large-congregation environment (800+), preferably with small groups.
- Demonstrated leadership and small-group facilitation skills.

Physical Requirements

- Able to move freely in and out of different small-group settings (homes, church, businesses).
- Able to speak in a public forum.

Core Competencies

Organizing. Can gather and organize resources (people, funding, material, support) to get things done; can orchestrate multiple activities at once to accomplish a goal; can use resources effectively and efficiently.

Planning. Accurately assesses the length and difficulty of a project; sets objectives and goals; breaks down work into process steps; develops schedules and task/people assignments; anticipates and adjusts for problems and roadblocks; measures performance against goals; evaluates results.

Managing vision and purpose. Articulates and supports the vision and mission of ABC church; communicates a compelling and inspired vision for ministry; talks beyond the here and now to a larger sense of purpose; creates a compelling vision of possibility, hope, and optimism; helps others to own the vision.

Developing volunteers. Is able to identify raw talent and recruit capable people into positions of responsibility; provides challenging and stretching tasks and assignments for others to do; delegates appropriately; builds people up; maintains open and active dialogue with volunteers; communicates expectations clearly and holds people accountable.

Managing conflict. Deals with problems quickly and directly; steps up to conflicts, seeing them as opportunities; reads situations quickly; focuses when listening; settles disputes collaboratively and equitably; finds common ground and gets cooperation.

Interpersonal relationships. Relates well to all kinds of people, inside and outside of the congregation; builds appropriate rapport; builds effective and constructive relationships; uses diplomacy and tact; is regarded as a team player.

Trust and integrity. Is widely trusted; seen as direct and truthful; keeps confidences; admits mistakes; adheres to an appropriate and effective set of core values during good and bad times; acts in line with those values; practices what he or she preaches.

Chapter 5

Hiring Right to Manage Easier

Israel asked for a king, and it was Samuel's job to identify one. Samuel consulted with God about the selection, and God said, "About this time tomorrow I will send you a man from the land of Benjamin. Anoint him leader over my people Israel." When Samuel caught sight of Saul, the Lord said to him, "This is the man I spoke to you about; he will govern my people" (1 Sam. 9:15-17).

Things could not have been much simpler for Samuel. God told Samuel specifically when the ideal candidate would show up and something about the candidate's background. Samuel didn't have to make any difficult decisions or discern what the ideal candidate would look like. He simply had to listen for the voice of God to tell him what to do next.

Most of us long for this kind of clarity in our hiring decisions. If God would just illuminate our way in the same way that God led Samuel, we would have no problem with staffing and supervision issues. In fact, many congregations can tell a story or two from their own memory banks about God-appointed leaders who showed up at mysteriously ordained moments, and everyone knew that this was the right person. More often than not, however, congregations have a much different kind of hiring experience. A job opening exists, congregational leaders have a pool of resumes, but no one seems to be rising to the top. Or a clear favorite seems to be emerging from the pool, but no one really knows for sure whether this candidate fits the congregation and the position. Or we excitedly hire a new employee, certain that this employee is just right for us, only to find out six months later what a terrible mistake we have made. We long for the clarity that God provided Samuel and Saul, but we live with uncertainty and confusion in the hiring process. Let's look at an example.

Bethel Church has an opening for an associate pastor. The search committee and pastor are frozen with indecision. The congregation has had two bad hires back to back, and the associate position has been vacant for three of the last five years. The first of the previous associates was technically very qualified for the position, but she was a poor match for the culture of the congregation. Becky continually tripped over "the way" to get things done at Bethel. Over time she alienated just about every lay leader in the congregation. Becky lasted fourteen months in the position.

Becky's successor, Jim, was well loved by church members but didn't have a passion for the basic skill sets of the position for which he had been hired. He was a great preacher and a gifted pastoral care provider, but the church was looking for an administrator to balance the skill set of the senior pastor. While Jim had some of these skills, he wasn't interested in a predominantly administrative role, even though he had expressed such an interest during the interview process. After nine months on the job, Jim left to pursue a ministry slot that was more consistent with his interests. A new search committee has been formed, but committee members and the senior pastor are understandably skittish about moving forward. What will prevent them from making yet another hiring mistake?

In Jim Collins's book *Good to Great*, Collins outlines five distinctives that separate good companies from truly great companies. According to Collins, the first distinctive is "First who . . . then what." We might expect that great leaders would be distinguished from other types of leaders by their ability to cast vision and define strategy. What Collins found instead is that great leaders always began with getting the right people onto the bus, the wrong people off the bus, and the right people in the right seats—and then they figured out where to drive the bus. The old adage "People are your most important asset" turns out to be wrong. People are not your most important asset. The *right* people are.[1]

Clearly the task of identifying the right staff members to serve on a staff team is one of the most critical decisions a congregation must make. Let's examine the most common pitfalls and mistakes that prevent congregations from getting the right people on their teams.

✳ Common Pitfalls ✳

A common spiritual pitfall that <u>many congregations make is</u> *the failure to see the hiring process as a spiritual process*. Selecting leadership for the church is a sacred task. Throughout Scripture God continually has something to say about the selection of leaders. The hiring process is the beginning of a new relationship between a prospective employee and your congregation. What could be more sacred? As such, the hiring process needs to be grounded in prayer, and those who participate in the hiring process need to be actively involved in discernment.

A more pragmatic pitfall that many congregations experience is *lack of clarity about what they are seeking*. Often a vague description of a position is identified, funding is procured, and the recruiting process begins. The congregation ends up finding a person they like with general skill sets in the category of competencies that are needed, and they hire that person, expecting that he or she will help to craft the job upon entering the organization. This is the congregation that says, "We know we have additional personnel needs in this area, and we want you to come in here and figure out what the job ought to look like as you find your way around." Sometimes this type of arrangement works out well, but more often it ends in profound disappointment on the part of the employee and the congregation. To avoid this pitfall, you will want to carefully consider the material presented in the chapters of this book on the importance of outcomes (chapter 3) and creating the job description (chapter 4). You <u>should never begin a hiring process until you have clarity about the job description, including the core competencies and essential functions of the position</u>. Furthermore, you should never begin a hiring process until the position has been fully approved by all appropriate bodies of the congregation that are constitutionally required to have a voice. Nothing will confuse a process and a potential candidate more than having the job description evolve in the midst of the hiring process.

A third common mistake that congregations make is *hiring in response to the availability of a specific candidate.* Leadership has a vague notion about a new position and is aware of someone "really good" who may not be available several months from now. Or leadership has defined a position well and begins a well-thought-out interview process but ditches the agreed upon time frames and procedures for hiring because the perfect candidate appears who is being courted by another employer. The congregation is convinced that they have to move now or are likely to lose the candidate. Hiring decisions made in haste almost always come back to haunt the congregation, either because the candidate wasn't really a good match to begin with or because the incoming candidate wasn't provided with clear expectations.

Churches tend to regret their hiring decisions when they fall into the trap of *hiring the opposite of a previous problem employee.* Maryanne had been a technically competent office manager, but she was difficult to work with one-on-one. Church members often reported that Maryanne was moody and very inclined to foster pet projects while ignoring things she wasn't interested in doing. After many frustrating years of dealing with Maryanne, the congregation's personnel committee decided to let Maryanne go. As a reaction against Maryanne's deficiencies, the personnel committee overemphasized interpersonal skills during the interview process at the expense of technical skills. Thom was hired to fill the role, primarily because of the warmth of his personality. Three months later Thom was fired when the committee realized that he had limited word processing and desktop publishing skills. A well-crafted interview process will insure that all the needed skill sets of a position are attended to during the hiring process.

Other congregations make the mistake of *hiring people primarily because they are "just like us."* In these situations the interview process focuses only minimally on the competencies of the position and instead focuses on the temperament or personality of the person.

When the hiring committee finds someone who thinks and talks like they do, they hire that person with the mistaken impression that he or she "belongs with us." This is how congregations often end up with a staff team made up exclusively of introverts or extroverts, thinkers or feelers, intuitives or sensors. Common sense tells us that a well-rounded staff includes a variety of temperament types and work approaches. A diverse team will work more creatively together and be better equipped to serve the full set of congregational needs. Yet somehow during the uncertainty of the interview process, we are comforted by meeting people just like us, and so we tend to hire sameness.

Often during an interview process congregational leaders will fall victim to the *halo effect.* The halo effect occurs when a hiring committee discovers one interesting or wonderful attribute in a candidate and lets that singular attribute distort their full impression of the person. St. Elizabeth's was hiring a youth minister. One of the candidates for the position, Mark, was a wonderful musician. He played the guitar well and had a very casual style that involved picking up the guitar and singing his way through a Bible study lesson. The interview committee loved this part of Mark. During each stage of the interview process, a member of the committee would introduce him by saying to an interviewer, "Make sure you ask Mark to play for you while you are talking to him." People were so enamored with Mark's impromptu guitar playing that they failed to look at his organizational and communication skills. The committee assumed that Mark's whimsical musical ways with the youth would be so endearing that he would operate as a sort of pied piper, attracting youth from miles around. Instead, Mark turned out to be very poorly organized. None of the programs that he talked about instituting ever materialized, and he continually alienated the parents of youth in the program through his failure to communicate. After several months the youth grew bored with Mark's simple guitar playing teaching style and congregational leaders were left with an incompetent employee.

A major interview error that congregations make is *hiring someone after only one interview.* To determine the fitness of a candidate, it is imperative that you see that person interact with a variety of people at a variety of different times and in different settings. The candidate that interviews well sitting in the office of the senior pastor may not interview as well when interacting with parishioners in someone's home. Don't worry about being redundant. Asking the candidate the same questions in different settings, among different people will allow you to compare notes and to check for consistency in the responses.

One of the worst mistakes that congregations make during the hiring process is a *failure to check references*. Reference checks will rarely tell you if this is the right person for the job. However, they are priceless when it comes to identifying people who are wrong for the job. The best people to provide you with an evaluation of a candidate are people who have worked with him or her before. They can provide invaluable insights into working style, strengths, and weaknesses. Why wouldn't you take advantage of this valuable resource? It's true that previous employers are often tight-lipped with information about an employee, particularly when they are concerned about the legality of sharing that information. But you can almost always glean some useful information, even if the best information you gather is the unstated "between the lines" signal that you can gather from inferences and intonations. Later in this chapter we will share some pointers for conducting a reference check.

The Hiring Process

The process that you engage in when you seek to hire a new employee is a profoundly spiritual endeavor. Each time you hire a new employee, you and your congregation are making a statement of hope, a statement that you believe in the future of your ministry and your congregation, a statement about new beginnings. Hiring a new employee requires abundance thinking—an affirmation that the financial condition of the church will be sufficient to provide for the well-being of that employee. The hiring process is about a potential employer and employee discussing mutual need and overlapping areas of giftedness. This requires vulnerability on the part of the congregation and potential candidates to speak genuinely with one another and to present themselves truthfully and honestly to one another. These are spiritual issues, and whatever hiring process you design needs to have a spiritual foundation. Yes, we need to engage in all of the pragmatic things that accompany a hiring process—job description, resumes, interviews, and reference checks. But, in a spiritually driven process, we will always recognize these things for what they are—tools of discipline that keep our focus clear and allow us to create a pathway for something more to occur. The entire hiring process needs to be a prayer-centered experience. Those whom you select to participate in an interviewing process need to be people of spiritual maturity and wisdom, with some openness to the notion that God may have something to say about your employment choices. So as you or others design a recruiting process, be intentional about the spiritual dimension of the tasks that lie ahead of you.

As already stated, the process of hiring someone always needs to begin with a full description of the position being filled. Chapter 4 on job descriptions will take you through all of the steps needed to define the position thoroughly. Do not attempt to read this chapter unless you have already read that one. As you are designing the position, you will also want to think carefully about all of the people who need to be involved in the hiring process. Denominational polities and constitutional guidelines must be considered when designing a hiring process. Even if your polity gives you full authority to select and hire a new staff employee, you will want to make certain that others are involved in making the selection along with you.

Bob is an Episcopal rector who is assured by his bishop and his polity that he has full authority to make all hiring and firing decisions in his congregation. But Bob is also politically savvy enough to know that others need to be involved in his hiring decisions. No priest, pastor, or rabbi should operate under the mistaken impression that his or her singular perspective is enough to spot all of the possible ways in which an employee may be a misfit. Multiple voices will help Bob insure that his chosen candidate is an excellent match for the position, the context, and the culture of the congregation.

Who should you involve in the hiring process? Generally, you need to insure that your governing board is aware of the process, and you will often want to include as least one member of the board as an interviewer. You will also want to incorporate the input of other staff members who will be able to help you determine if the person will work well within the culture of your staff. Finally, it is good to get the input of someone who will be considered a member of this employee's constituent group (e.g., a member of the youth group when hiring a youth pastor). Remember that you want the interview team to be composed of people with wisdom and spiritual openness.

Once the new position has been fully authorized and you have identified the appropriate people to involve in the hiring decisions, you can begin to assemble a pool of candidates. Try to assemble a respectable pool of candidates before you begin the interview process. Evaluating candidates who are in the same stages of a hiring process allows you to do a better job of comparison and contrast. Sharon has already had two interviews with one candidate for an opening on her staff. Two more resumes of potential candidates have just arrived on her desk. Sharon may have some difficulty comparing the attributes of the newly surfaced candidates with the candidate she has already interviewed. A staggered start to the recruitment process may be unavoidable, but Sharon will be better off to the extent that she can postpone starting any interviews until she has a well-developed pool of candidates.

After a pool of potential candidates has been assembled, it is often helpful to sort through a stack of resumes by using a simple force ranking system. Create three piles of candidates: those who look like a strong match for the position (your A list candidates), those who may be a match but demonstrate some gaps (your B list candidates), and those who clearly are not a fit (your C list candidates). Immediately send a letter to your C list candidates to thank them for applying and to let them know that they are not being considered for the position. If the candidate pool is fairly shallow, invite your A and B list candidates in for a first interview. If the candidate pool is deep and/or you have limited resources for interviewing, invite your A candidates in immediately and hold off on inviting your B candidates. If you decide not to interview your B candidates immediately, make sure that you make some form of contact with them to let them know that you are interested in them as candidates but are not able to schedule interviews with them quite yet.

The first round of interviews ought to focus on determining if the candidates have the qualifications needed to meet the essential functions of the position. Do they meet the educational requirements of the position? Do they have the experience and skills required to perform the essential functions of the position? In the first interview you should not try to determine whether a candidate has the core competencies (demonstrated behavior standards) to serve in this role, and you should not be overly concerned with how well he or she will fit with other members of the team. You are simply trying to figure out if the candidate has the basics to do the job. For this reason, you don't necessarily need to have your first-round candidates speak with every member of the recruiting team. A conversation with one or two members of the hiring team ought to allow the basic first-round assessment. A half hour interview is generally sufficient to find out what you need to know. This first interview may take place by telephone or in person. Make certain that you design your interview questions ahead of time so that you are not just improvising as you go along during the interview.

A candidate will pass successfully through the first round of interviews if the interviewer(s) determines that he or she meets the minimum requirements to do the job and on some level appears to be a fit with the congregation. All candidates who fulfill this basic designation will be asked back for a second round of interviews. During the second round of interviews, you will want to make certain that all designated members of the hiring team talk with the candidates one-on-one. Group interviews at this stage are rarely effective and tend to intimidate even the best of candidates. During the second stage of interviewing, you are trying to evaluate the candidate's fit with the congregation, the staff, and with the specific position available. These interviews tend to be longer in duration (one hour) so that you can sufficiently explore the core competencies of the candidate and evaluate the candidate's fit with your culture. To the extent possible, you will want to schedule these interviews back to back on the same day so that the candidate does not have to make repeated trips to your location. Make certain to schedule break times into the day for both interviewers and the interviewee. Interviewing is an exhausting task, and no one can do it for six to eight hours straight. Again, design your interview format ahead of time.

When all of the second interviews have been completed, assemble your interviewing team for feedback and evaluation. Begin this session with some type of spiritual practice that makes sense for your tradition. As the group discusses the various candidates, you should avoid having them talk about who they "liked" and who they "didn't like." Such conversations are rarely productive and can degenerate into gossip. Rather, talk your way through the job description. Which candidate(s) could fulfill the essential functions of the position? Which candidate(s) demonstrated the core competencies required? Which candidate(s) would fit within our culture? Any candidate whose name is offered in response to all three questions should be placed on the final candidate list.

At this point in the interview process, your list of possible candidates should have narrowed considerably. Hopefully you still have two or three names on your list. If none of your candidates makes it through the second round of evaluation, you will need to go back to the drawing board and begin assembling another pool of candidates to interview. Assuming that you still have candidates to work with, this is the place in the process when you conduct your reference checks. Ask each candidate to submit the names of three references you can contact. References should be checked by telephone rather than e-mail. You can glean a great deal from intonation of voice and pregnant pauses over the phone that you can't gather from any type of written correspondence. Make certain that the candidate(s) know you are in the process of contacting their references so that the candidate(s) has sufficient opportunity to notify the references that you intend to contact them.

Before you pick up the phone to contact a reference, spend some time working on your own frame of mind. During the call you want to be open to hearing whatever it is that the reference wants to say to you. If you are already convinced that you are going to hire this person, the reference will hear that in your voice and will not be inclined to share concerns or cautions as openly. You are not calling to justify a decision to hire or not hire. You are simply using this conversation as one additional piece of evidence in your hiring decision process. Be open. Ask open-ended questions. Take notes during the conversation to force yourself to really hear what is being said. Ask follow-up questions in response to comments made.

Most references will be open and willing to speak with you. Some will be operating under policies and constraints established by their employers that limit what they can say. Following is a list of helpful questions to ask during a reference check. These are questions that most people can and will answer.

- What is your relationship to the candidate? What is the context in which you know him/her?
- How long have you known him/her?
- If the reference is an employer (previous or current) ask him or her to verify the dates of employment that were provided to you on the candidate's resume.
- Describe the key responsibilities that he/she assumed in his/her most recent position.
- What was his/her most important contribution to your organization?
- What kind of attitude and outlook did he/she bring into the work space?
- What kind of environment does he/she work best in?
- How would you describe his/her relationship with others?
- Describe his/her productivity and his/her commitment to quality and to his/her constituents.
- Would you hire him/her again if you had the chance?

Provide the reference with a brief (two or three sentences) description of the position that is open. Then ask the following questions:

- What strengths and abilities do you think he/she will bring to this position?
- What liabilities or weaknesses will he/she need to work on to successfully fill a role like this one?

- Is there anything else that we should know about him/her before making a hiring decision?

After completion of the reference checks, you may decide that you are ready to make a hiring decision. For certain kinds of positions, you may feel the need to conduct an additional round of interviews. This is particularly important for positions that require interaction with a target group of the congregation, such as youth, children, or senior adults. A third round of interviews may bring the candidate into a group context in a member's home for a meal or small group gathering. During this round of the interview process, you can watch the candidate interact with the constituency group that he or she will minister to or work with. The small group can informally pose questions and assess the candidate's interaction with the target constituency. Once your candidate(s) has been evaluated at each of these levels, you should be ready to make an employment decision.

Throughout the interview process, it is important to keep in regular contact with all of the candidates in your open pool. As soon as you know that a candidate is no longer a viable choice for your position, you should let that candidate know with a written letter that he or she is no longer being considered for the position. All other candidates should be contacted occasionally to let them know that they are still in the running for the position and when they are likely to be contacted next. Even candidates whom you are not actively considering but don't want to fully dismiss yet need to be contacted on an ongoing basis. The hiring process is a highly anxious time for your candidates. Do them the courtesy of letting them know where things are so that they can be about the business of planning their lives and their work. You certainly don't want to alienate someone you are interested in having join your organization by ignoring him or her for long periods of time as you run your process.

Christ Church spent eighteen months in dialogue with their candidate with very little contact for long periods of time. By the time they got around to offering the candidate the job, she decided that she didn't want to work for them. The way a potential employee is treated during the interview process is often a signal about how he or she will be treated as an employee. Make sure that the impression you generate is a positive one.

Similarly, it is important for you to be in prayer for and about the candidates throughout the process. These candidates are considering making a major life change to join your ministry. Even the conversations about the possibility of employment are an act of risk for them. Remember the candidates and their families in your prayer life and in the prayer life of your congregation.

Finally, let us offer a word about employment testing. Certain positions will require competency in a skill base area that you, as an interviewer, are not qualified to assess. Perhaps the employee needs to demonstrate proficiency with certain software or technology. A variety of written and online testing tools are available to test the skill base of potential employees in an objective manner. If you choose to use one of these tools, you need to make certain that the tool has been validated through research, and you need to insure that the tool is testing for skills that are considered essential functions of the job. Refusing to hire someone because they do not have a skill set that turns out to be nonessential to the job is illegal.

Forms of the Interview

There are four widely used interview types: traditional, situational, case, and behavior-based. Each of these interview types is appropriate for assessing different types of skills and competencies. Each can be used effectively at different points in the interview process. The most commonly used forms of interviewing in congregational contexts are the traditional and the behavior-based interview.

Traditional interviews tend to focus on questions that are leading or are resume- and background-based. Examples: Tell me about yourself. What are your strengths? What are your weaknesses? Why should we hire you? Where do you want to be five years from now? Traditional interview questions are most useful in the first round of interviews during which you are trying to learn the basic facts about a potential employee.

Situational interviews put candidates into hypothetical situations. They may start out with "How would you. . . ?" or "What would you do if. . . ?" You can use the situational interview in a second or third round interview if you have a specific context in mind that the candidate is likely to encounter if hired for this position. Remember, simply because a candidate can respond well to a situational interview doesn't mean that he or she will necessarily be able to respond as well in a real-life situation. Some people are very good at talking about a situation but quite ineffective when it comes to acting on the situation. Nevertheless, a situational interview approach can help you identify something about the candidate's philosophy of work and ministry.

Case interviews involve presenting the candidate with a hypothetical case and asking the candidate to think out loud so that the direction of thinking becomes apparent. They are very similar to situation interviews. In a situational interview the candidate is asked to place himself or herself in the situation and comment on what he or she would do. In the case interview the candidate is invited to observe the situation from a more detached, outside perspective. The candidate is asked to analyze the problem, ask pertinent questions, evaluate the situation, and propose solutions and conclusions. A case interview question helps to identify how a candidate frames a problem statement and diagnoses a problem situation. In the process of solving the case, the candidate is sharing his or her logic process and decision-making criteria with you.

Behavior-based interviews can be distinguished from other interview formats in five ways:[2]

- You ask the candidate to describe how he/she actually *did* behave in a particular situation, rather than how he/she *would* behave. Behavior-based interviewing rests on the premise that past performance is the best predictor of future success. Unlike case interviews, which are purely hypothetical, a behavior-based interview focuses on actual behaviors that the candidate chose to apply in previous situations.

- You ask an initial question, then follow up with several probing questions. You keep digging to get at the core of the story.
- You ask the candidate for details so that he or she can't theorize, fabricate, or generalize answers.
- The interview is a structured process focusing on predetermined competencies, giving you more control and direction so that you don't go off course with irrelevant conversation.
- You take structured notes to document facts so that later you can rate all of your candidates accurately against consistent standards.

Behavior-based interviewing is the best of the four interview approaches for assessing core competencies. You will remember that core competencies are the established standards of behavior expected to successfully fill the position. Asking people to talk about other times and situations in which they demonstrated these competencies is the best way to assess their fit with the job. Behavior-based interviewing is most effectively used in the second round of interviews when you are trying to assess the competencies and congregational fit.

To prepare for a behavior-based interview, you will need to establish questions to extract the desired core competencies.

Here are some examples of behavior-based interview questions:

- Describe an instance when you had to think on your feet to extricate yourself from a difficult situation.
- Give me a specific example of a time when you used good judgment and logic in solving a problem.
- Describe a time when time limitations forced you to choose between completing two very important pastoral tasks. What criteria did you use to make your choice?
- Describe a time when you had to use written communication skills to get an important point across.

- Give me an example of a time when you were able to successfully communicate with another person even when that individual may not have liked you (or vice versa).
- Tell of a time when you worked with a staff member who was not completing his or her share of the work.
- Describe a situation in which you had to arrive at a compromise or guide others to a compromise.
- Tell about a time when you had to resolve a conflict between two staff members or two board members. What approach did you take?
- Tell of some situations in which you have had to adjust quickly to changes over which you had no control. What was the impact of the change on you?
- Describe some times when you were not very satisfied or pleased with your performance. What did you do about it?

Structuring an Interview

When it comes to actually structuring an interview, you will want to make certain that you carefully organize your time so that you have the capacity to ask the questions you need to ask, the candidate has time to ask questions that he or she has, and you can establish a proper tone for the overall interview. Following is a sample format for a sixty-minute interview. Note that each stage of the interview has a specific purpose.[3]

Introduction (3–5 minutes)

During this time you are seeking to:

- build rapport
- provide background information about the position and the congregation
- communicate expectations about the interview process

Interviewer's Questions/Candidate's Answers (45 minutes)

- Start out with your traditional questions using the candidate's resume as a guide. Find out the basics you need to know about his/her background.
- Devote at least 25 minutes to behavior-based questions addressing the competencies of the position you have identified.
- Pace yourself according to the number of competencies you have identified.
- Make sure the candidate does most of the talking during this time.
- Control the interview.
- Probe for information.
- Take descriptive notes.
- Save evaluative work for after the interview.

Candidate's Questions (10 minutes)

Most candidates will have prepared questions to show that they are very interested in the position. Save enough time to let them ask their questions. You can tell a great deal about a candidate by the quality of the questions they ask you.

Interview Close (3–5 minutes)

- Sell the ministry position.
- Sell the congregation.
- Communicate next steps.

The hiring process can be a highly stressful time that you struggle to get through so that you can begin an employment relationship, or it can be a spiritually rich beginning of a new relationship with a future employee. Careful attention to the overall process and careful crafting of interview design will keep your process engaging and productive for you and for your potential employees.

Chapter 6

Supervision as Performance Management

"Now as an elder myself and a witness of the sufferings of Christ, as well as one who shares in the glory to be revealed, I exhort the elders among you to tend the flock of God that is in your charge, exercising the *oversight*, not under compulsion but willingly as God would have you do it—not for sordid gain but eagerly."
                    1 Peter 5:1-2 NRSV (emphasis added)

Oversight has always been seen as both a gift to be exercised in the faith community and a responsibility of the elder leader. In episcopal denominations the notion of oversight *(episkope)* carries the full authority of Scripture in the role of bishop and by extension to those who stand for the bishop in times of his or her absence. The expectation is that the senior leader will provide oversight for others in their work and lives. The purpose is to express and promote essential unity in the body of the community to fulfill its call.

Nonetheless, there are few roles more problematic to senior clergy who are responsible for oversight of their staff—or, by extension, of those who have oversight responsibilities for others. Supervision commonly is seen as time consuming and often experienced as taking on someone else's troubles and problems—when the leader may feel that he or she has sufficient troubles and problems of his or her own. Many of the dilemmas involved in supervision stem from less than helpful ideas of the purpose of this leadership role. To that end, it may be helpful to begin by noting some ideas of what supervision is *not* meant to be. While any of the roles and strategies noted below may be necessary or appropriate in a given situation or time, these are not the dominant or most helpful approaches to supervision.

What Supervision Is *Not*

Supervision Is Not Direction or Control

Supervision is not telling someone what to do or how to do his or her work. To approach supervision of staff from the perspective of having to direct their work is exhausting to senior clergy, who appropriately would rather not have to get involved in the day-to-day details and responsibilities of others. To use supervision as the platform to tell others how to do their work limits the creativity and commitment of others who receive such direction. By creating a situation in which staff must wait for the direction of the senior clergy, the work of the congregation also is limited to what the senior clergy can himself or herself master and direct. Directing people under supervision is a tiring task, which, by its nature, limits the ministry rather than extends it. It leads to the situation where "the leader runs out of time while those supervised run out of work." The staff cannot extend beyond the limits of the direction of the person under whom they serve.

Supervision Is Not Shared Work

While the supervisor is not the director who initiates strategies and activities, as noted above, the supervisor also is not the problem solver who can do and direct what others cannot figure out. The supervisory meeting is not a time to share work and engage the leader in doing the work or solving the problems brought to him or her by the staff member being supervised. One of the essential tasks of leaders is to give the work back to the people to whom it belongs.

In one of the most frequently requested reprints of an article from the *Harvard Business Review*, authors William Oncken and

Donald Wass use the image of a monkey on a worker's back. The idea is that if a leader meets—formally or informally—with a staff member to discuss that person's work and, at the end of the conversation, the leader has something more to do, the leader has allowed the staff member to take the "work monkey" off of his or her own back and put it on the leader's back. One of the temptations of all leaders is to take and care for too many monkeys that belong to other workers. This may be especially true of clergy who by vocation and often by personality seek to be—and feel rewarded when—they are helpful to anyone with a problem.

Instead, the task of the leader is to engage another staff member who is wrestling with his or her own work and to have conversations to explore ideas, solutions, and strategies. At the end of the conversation, the leader is to return to his or her own work without additional responsibilities that belong to the staff member. In turn, if the conversation has been managed well, the staff member will leave with a new idea to try, a new resource to pursue, or renewed energy and commitment to return to the task. In this case, the monkey has been kept where it belongs—as the responsibility of the staff member. The leader was engaged and listened and resourced the staff member but did not inappropriately share the work that belonged to the staff member.

Supervision Is Not the Leader's Chance to "Improve" the Staff Member

In chapter 1, one of the four assumptions that Buckingham and Coffman of the Gallup Organization argue must be broken is the notion that people can achieve anything to which they set their mind. This assumption encourages supervisors to set themselves to the task of improving or "fixing" staff members under their supervision. Time is spent trying to make a spontaneous staff member more organized and structured or an organized and structured staff member more spontaneous. Supervision poorly understood will find a leader suggesting ways for staff to amend their personalities or to practice organizational and spiritual gifts they do not have. Personal and professional development is a hallmark of good professional behavior and of a faithful Christian or Jewish life. Finding our way continually into a deepened heart, ever-maturing behavior, and extension of our gifts is a part of the discipline of a commitment of faith. However, it is not the appropriate goal of a supervisory relationship for the leader to direct the development of an individual staff member in any of these ways. In fact, organizational consultant and theologian-philosopher Peter Block, in his discussion of leadership as an exercise of stewardship rather than as control of an organization, strongly suggests that to direct and control the development of others in the workplace is an act of patriarchy.[2]

Later, as we explore what appropriate supervision is, we will return to the need for the personal and professional development of staff. But at the moment it is sufficient to note that supervision is not an exercise in a leader's changing or developing a staff member to be more productive, competent, or mature.

Supervision Is Not Therapy or Pastoral Care

Supervision is not a counseling or pastoral care session in which life issues are explored or in which the staff member seeks personal encouragement or counsel from the leader. People want their work to be meaningful and to make a difference. People hope work will be a pleasant and energizing experience. But to assume that we are to be personally nurtured by our work, our workplace, or our supervisor is inappropriate. Thomas Cooley, dean of the Stern School of Business at New York University, addressed graduating students, saying, "You can hope to love your job, but you can never hope that your job will love you."[3] The task of supervision is not to care for the staff person, although supervision can never be uncaring. The goal of supervision demands a focus on the work, not on the person. Staff are resources for ministry.

Supervision Is Not (Summative) Evaluation

Evaluation is a difficult topic in congregations for a multitude of reasons that we will explore briefly later. It too easily is thought of as a judgment of whether a person is good or bad, effective or ineffective. In fact, there are two kinds of evaluation—summative and formative:[4]

- Summative evaluation moves toward a conclusion, a judgment: How well is this staff person advancing the overall mission of this congregation? *or* Is this the right person for the job?
- Formative evaluation helps the staff person move ahead: What changes and enhancements can be made to aid the staff person in advancing the overall mission of this congregation?

The supervision meeting is not usually a summative conversation focused on how well or how poorly the staff person is doing. While this may certainly be a part of a larger overall performance review for a staff person, such summative conclusions are not the purpose of the supervisory meeting and often are not helpful. As will be noted later, the process of supervision more appropriately expresses formative evaluation: What does this person need to move ahead? What changes need to be made to set this person free to move toward the wanted outcome? What questions, if asked, will help this person learn more or think creatively about the task?

Supervision as Performance Management

In a continuing education event, Susan pointed out that the appropriate object of supervision is a verb, not a noun. A person is a noun. When senior pastors think of themselves as supervising a noun, they easily fall into the traps noted above, focusing too easily on the staff member. Attention is drawn to what the staff person is doing (controlling and directing activities), what the staff person needs to change about himself or herself, and how to make the staff person happy and productive at the same time.

More appropriately the object of supervision is a verb—the work being done. What is being supervised is the *performance* of the staff member as he or she works toward identified outcomes, not the person. The distinction between noun and verb, between person and performance, is helpful as a backdrop to identifying what supervision *is*.

Instead of simply listing characteristics of what good supervision is as a counterpoint to the above list of what supervision is not, let us return to the questions, noted in chapter 1 of this resource, that the Gallup Organization has identified as the key measures of the strength of a workplace. These questions identify what workers look for and need in their workplace in order to find meaning in their work and to feel challenged to be productive. These questions offer a framework for considering what good supervision is. Focus will be given to the top six questions Gallup identifies as the most powerful drivers for staff.[5]

Question 1: Do I Know What Is Expected of Me at Work?

Supervision is about clear outcomes. Staff need clarity about the specific outcomes of ministry for which they are responsible and will be held accountable. As noted in chapter 3 on outcomes, congregations are notorious for being unclear about what they are called to produce. Such lack of clarity puts staff members in the difficult position of not being sure how to direct their efforts and attention while being subject to multiple preferences and pressures from the people with whom they work. It is the responsibility of the senior clergy, working with the governing board, first to bring clarity to the mission of the whole congregation and then to bring clarity of expectations and outcomes to the work of the individual staff members as those efforts support the overall mission. Staff need clarity at two levels:

- For what am I specifically responsible?
- How does my work and my output fit into and contribute to the larger mission and ministry of the whole congregation?

Bringing clarity to the work of the staff is a critical part of what is commonly referred to as the *visioning task* of the senior leader. Again, working with the board, it is the senior leader who needs to shape the conversation and lead the discernment around the call and the mission of the congregation and then align all efforts, staff, and other resources to that vision.

Being clear about outcomes with individual staff members is critical to accountability. Staff need to know specifically about what they will be asked. Knowing that they will be asked about express outcomes will direct their attention to those outcomes, and their efforts will focus on achieving the identified results. This is an issue of organizational alignment that is managed by the way in which the senior leader focuses his or her attention. What the leader focuses on matters, because the rest of the organization will follow where the leader places attention.

The 1983 movie *Blue Thunder* offered an example of organizational alignment directed by the leader's attention. The film's main focus was an urban assault helicopter, a very high-tech helicopter designed to fly into highly congested urban areas where there was rioting or violence. The idea was that the pilot could fly into such dense and chaotic territory and be able to fire upon the "bad" people while not firing on the "good" people. The idea of such a helicopter is both frightening (since such helicopters do apparently exist) and offensive, since it represents maximum force to be used against people struggling with their own chaos. The key, however, by which the helicopter could distinguish between "good" and "bad" people was located in the pilot's helmet. All of the armaments of the helicopter were tied into the pilot's helmet so that wherever the pilot looked, from right to left, up or down, the guns would follow. Simply by looking at a target, the pilot was effectively aiming the full force of the helicopter in one place. This is a chilling prospect but an excellent example of a system's alignment.

Congregations, organizations, and communities align themselves to the place where the leader gives his or her attention. Staff align their efforts to those places where their supervisor will make inquiries about progress and learning.

Question 2: Do I Have the Materials and Equipment I Need to Do My Work Right? and . . .

Question 3: At Work, Do I Have the Opportunity to Do What I Do Best Every Day?

Supervision is about resourcing. Supervisory time provides opportunity to do careful listening about the development of a staff person's work and to test if the person has—or needs to find—the resources necessary to produce the outcomes for which he or she will be held accountable. It is neither productive nor just to ask a person to produce a result but not provide the needed resources. The typical resources necessary to produce results include the following:

- time
- dollars
- information
- training
- support of others through conversation
- support of others through prayer
- support of others through participation

Senior clergy commonly have a responsibility to inquire about and keep an eye on the resources available to support the work of staff persons. This may mean inquiring about the budget for a given program or working with the finance committee to redirect funds toward a program. It may mean suggesting that the staff person give more time in one area of work while explaining to people that other areas of the staff person's work will receive less attention and participation.

Information and training are often critical resources for senior clergy to keep an eye on in times of supervision because we are in an in-between time of learning. Many congregations and staff have discovered that what has been normative practice no longer works—or at least does not get the same results. At the same time, it is not clear in many areas of ministry what will work, particularly when a question is raised within the unique context of an individual congregation. Such an in-between moment requires learning and experimentation. Because this is an in-between time and because the senior clergy is supervising work in an area for which he or she is not personally providing leadership, there is no reason to think that the senior clergy will have the information or answers that others do not have or can personally provide the training needed. Nonetheless, the senior clergy is responsible to note when new ideas and new resources are needed and when new strategies and experiments need to be developed. Calling the staff person's attention to the need for new ideas and strategies is appropriate supervisory action by the senior clergy.

For instance, one senior clergy whom Gil was coaching was supervising a staff member responsible for working with the youth of the church and the community. The history of youth work in this congregation and the learned style of the youth worker were content rich and very educational in style. Much of the time was spent in classroom settings, teaching about faith formation and congregational membership. However, the youth staff member was making slow progress in group formation, experiential learning, and straightforward relationship building. Several attempts to address these issues were tried with minimal results, and it was clear that the staff worker needed to learn something new in order to move ahead. The senior clergy was not clear on what needed to be learned. Nonetheless, in supervision the issue of additional resources of information and training was raised, and the senior clergy asked that by the next time they talked, the youth worker report with whom (within or outside the congregation) she had talked to discover what was needed to move ahead. The youth worker also agreed that by the next conversation with the senior clergy, she would present a list of resources and training experiences she felt she would need to break out into the "new." Resources were being provided even though the staff person needed to identify and locate them herself.

Resourcing also plays a large part in noting whether particular pieces of work are eliciting or draining a worker's enthusiasm and energy. We are most energized when we are doing what we do best and what we believe to be most important. That does not mean that any of us has the experience of working only within the "best and most important." Everyone's job and everyone's day are a mix of things that energize and drain, that excite and exhaust. Supervision, however, allows the senior clergy to listen for when a staff person (a resource of the congregation) is being misused because he or she is deflated by working in areas where others have better energy, skills, and enthusiasm. It is a part of resourcing to talk with staff about how they will apply themselves to the parts of the task for which they are best suited and well skilled and how they might enlist others to collaborate in areas that drain and deflate them.

Question 4: In the Last Seven Days, Have I Received Recognition or Praise for Doing Good Work? and . . .

Question 5: Does My Supervisor, or Someone at Work, Seem to Care about Me as a Person?

Supervision is about recognition and accountability. There is little worse than working hard and having no one notice the effort or the results. Recently Gil spent a full morning working on a memo in which he attempted to identify some hard-won insights, and sent it off to some people who were working with him on the project. After a week he still had not received a response to the memo. Gil knew that these colleagues may still have been thinking about the memo in order to form a response, or that the memo simply may not have made it to the top of the considerable piles of issues for which they are responsible. But the emotional—and much more personal—effect was to make Gil feel devalued. His enthusiasm for new learnings began to drop sharply.

A major part of the "care" a staff person needs in supervision is the simple demonstration that the senior clergy (and other leaders when the senior clergy can honestly report it) is aware and appreciative of what the staff person is doing. This is especially true when any notable progress in the work has been made. Surprisingly, this part of the work of supervision is simple—as simple as remembering what was last talked about and planned and then inquiring about what has happened since. Nevertheless, this supervisory conversation can be very powerful for the following reasons.

First, power comes simply from the awareness that someone is paying attention and focusing attention on the staff person's work. By itself, directing attention increases effort and productivity. This is known as the "Hawthorne effect."[6] In a 1939 study of how varied levels of lighting in a manufacturing plant affected production, it was determined that the increase in production was caused as much or more by the simple fact that the workers whose areas received increased lighting felt the attention of management than it was caused by the additional lighting.

Second, attention given to an intention also produces accountability. If the staff person knows that he or she is going to be asked about an agreed-upon task, it is much more likely that the task will be addressed. Gil frequently tells the story of a consultant friend who, upon reaching his fortieth birthday, gave himself the gift of tap-dancing lessons—something he had long wanted to do. The friend, however, immediately was discouraged when he found that everyone else in his tap-dancing class was female and under thirteen years of age. Because he really wanted to learn how to tap dance (and this class was his best opportunity to do so), on the evening of his first lesson, he wrote letters to his ten closest friends, inviting them to the recital at the end of the class. For sixteen weeks, every time he bumped into any of those friends, he was asked how "it" was going. The "it" in the simple question of "How's it going, Bob?" for those sixteen weeks was clearly the dancing class. The friend reported that he rarely felt so supported in something he was doing and so accountable to complete the lessons. With all that attention, there was no way he was not going to finish what he set out to do.

Third, inquiry and attention are often received as rewards. It is common to think of rewards as tangible and to think that the size or value of the reward makes a difference in impact. The power of a reward, however, is much more directly related to its intention and timing. The closer the reward is to the recognized event, the more value it carries. At the Foxboro Company, a technical advance was desperately needed for the company to survive its early days. Late one evening a scientist rushed into the president's office with a working prototype. It was just what they needed to keep the business afloat. Dumbfounded at the elegance of the solution and bemused about how to reward it, the president bent forward in his chair, rummaged through his desk drawers, found something, leaned over the desk to the scientist, and said, "Here!" In his hand was a banana—the only reward he immediately could put his hands on. From that point on, a small "gold banana" lapel pin has been the highest accolade for scientific achievement at Foxboro.[7]

Question 6: Is There Someone at Work Who Encourages My Development?

Supervision is about challenge. We noted earlier that supervision is not about "fixing" staff members or directing their development (i.e., making them better people or workers). To assume that the senior clergy knows what a person needs to do with his or her personal or professional life is patriarchal, as described by Peter Block. It is, however, the senior clergy's supervisory responsibility and opportunity to bring attention to opportunities and moments of development to help the staff person be aware and feel challenged. Not all opportunities will be taken, and some suggestions may not even be seen as welcome opportunities. Nonetheless, we all want to develop, to be more, to deepen our lives, and to find greater meaning. The supervisory moment is a prime opportunity to challenge the staff person to be more and to offer the encouragement that will provide support for the staff person's response to the challenge.

How Would a Supervision (Performance Management) Meeting Look?

Having considered the purpose of supervision, we now turn our attention to translating purpose into practice. Senior clergy are responsible to assure that a process is in place—a system is built—that can be used to align the work of staff through supervision. The style, the timing, and the level of formality of the supervisory meeting must be consistent with the people participating and with the culture of the congregation where it will be practiced. The following model is offered with an awareness that it needs to be tailored to the congregation and persons involved. (Senior clergy also can adapt and adopt some form of this model as a way to have a supervisory conversation with the personnel committee, the president of the congregation, the governing board, or whoever supervises and holds the senior clergy accountable for his or her work in the congregation.)

The form of this performance planning meeting comes from *First Break All the Rules: What the World's Greatest Managers Do Differently*, which, as noted earlier, Marcus Buckingham and Curt Coffman based on in-depth interviews that the Gallup Organization conducted with more than eighty thousand managers in more than four hundred companies. For a performance planning meeting, the person being supervised is encouraged to respond to the following questions in writing and use the written responses as the basis of the conversation.

The Agenda

A review of the past three months:

- What actions have you taken? These should be the details of performance over the past three months. The staff person should briefly include appropriate details and specifics.
- What discoveries have you made? This should be an account of formal and informal learning done in the past three months. What are the new insights, and from where did they come?
- What partnerships have you built? What new relationships have been built, or what old relationships have been strengthened? It is important that the staff person take responsibility for building his or her network of relationships.

A forecast of the next three months:

- What is your main focus? What are the primary goals that will get your priority attention over the next three months?
- What are you planning to learn over the next three months?
- What new partnerships (new relationships or strengthening of old relationships) are you hoping to build over the next three months?

The Supervisory Cycle

- Regularly scheduled every two to three months.
- The meeting commonly lasts thirty to forty-five minutes (The first one-third of the meeting focuses on the past, and the second two-thirds focus on what will be done in the period of time until the next conversation.)

Preparation and Response

- The staff person prepares for the conversation by providing written notes to the senior clergy that outline responses to the topics above.
- The written notes are shared with the senior clergy in advance of the conversation.
- The senior clergy drafts a brief (one page) written response memo within forty-eight hours, noting issues of agreement from the conversation, as well as topics that should be revisited in the subsequent performance management conversation.

Part of a Larger, Structured Working Relationship

The supervisory performance planning meeting is a part of a larger relationship in which the senior clergy works with other staff. This larger working relationship includes:

- daily side-by-side work that naturally keeps a conversation going between coworkers about the immediate task at hand
- weekly staff meetings where staff share information and where work is shaped and aligned
- occasional meetings requested by the supervisor or the staff worker about a specific topic or item
- an annual performance review

Chapter 7

Delegation

Knowing When and How to Set Work Free

Delegation involves passing on meaningful responsibility for the successful delivery of a task to other people while retaining an appropriate level of control over the process and the finished work.[1] Delegation does not overtly direct or control; neither does it abdicate or abandon.

Delegation can strengthen the life of a congregation in a number of significant ways. First, it may enhance the quality of leadership decision making. When a staff member or a volunteer lay leader has more expertise in how to do a task than others, he or she should be empowered to make related decisions. Or perhaps the nature of the staff person's work requires quick decisions in response to rapid changes in the environment. Allowing people to assume more responsibility for a task encourages them to become more responsive to their environment.

Delegation builds the capabilities of staff members. Senior staff leaders need to develop and grow the leadership capabilities of those on staff. Delegation allows the senior pastor to teach subordinates controlled portions of a larger job without overwhelming them with too much responsibility all at once.

Delegation provides a motivating environment for staff. The appropriate delegation of tasks can act to stimulate growth and enrichment, making ministry more interesting, challenging, and meaningful.

Delegation produces greater decision-making buy-in. People will work more diligently toward the successful implementation of a project or task when they have been part of the decision-making process.

Finally, through delegation the senior pastor can be freed for other important tasks. Delegation is an important time-management tool. By delegating less important duties and functions to others, senior leaders will free time for more important responsibilities. Even if the senior pastor could do the delegated task better or faster than someone else, it may be more effective for him or her to spend time on functions that will have the greatest impact on the life of the congregation.[2]

While delegation promises great potential for congregational growth and development, all too often those opportunities fail to materialize. Staff members fail to grasp what it is they are supposed to be doing, or they deliver work that is unacceptable and the senior staff member ends up doing the work anyway. Or the senior pastor delegates a task, and the staff member takes on more authority than was intended, creating havoc in the congregation. There are a variety of ways for delegation relationships to turn sour. Consider the following case.

Jim was worn out. First Church had grown by leaps and bounds during his seven-year tenure as head of staff. It had been an exciting and stressful ride. For some time it had been clear to Jim that the congregation was outgrowing its facility, but the congregational leadership did not want to deal with that hard reality by considering a building project. The sanctuary comfortably seated three hundred in worship, and each time worship attendance approached this magic number, the leadership responded by adding an additional worship service.

First Church now had two packed Sunday morning worship services and a Saturday night service that was growing. Jim typically delivered the message at all three services, and it was beginning to wear on him and his family. The addition of the Saturday night service had been particularly stressful. Saturday no longer felt like a day of rest or recreation, and his family was increasingly resentful when he withdrew from family activities to return to church by midafternoon. Additionally, the Saturday night crowd was a very different demographic than the Sunday morning communities. The congregants were more relaxed, informal, and always pushing him to introduce more in the way of contemporary worship music and themes. This was not Jim's area of strength, and he increasingly felt outside his comfort zone with the Saturday evening community.

So Jim was relieved when the personnel committee finally completed its work and hired a new associate pastor, Lynne, whose primary focus would be to plan and lead the Saturday evening service. Jim knew that Lynne would provide much better leadership than he ever could, and he gladly gave her full control of the reins. He introduced Lynne to the faith community and then stepped back and let her do her thing. Lynne was eager and willing, and Jim's life immediately felt better. A few small glitches occurred in the beginning, but within six weeks the Saturday worship community seemed happy and attendance was thriving.

Twelve weeks after Lynne's arrival, Jim began to receive visits from some of the longstanding members of the congregation, who were questioning the theological soundness of Lynne's teaching. Jim reassured people of his support for Lynne and their need to give her room to shape the ministry as she desired. Fifteen weeks into the assignment, he began to hear from members of his trustee group that Lynne was spending way outside the limits provided by the budget. He met with Lynne to talk about the problem and then reassured the trustees that things were taken care of. Twenty-four weeks into the new assignment, a growing rift began to emerge between the Saturday night worshiping community and the Sunday morning worshiping community. A host of complaints emerged, mostly focused on the condition in which the building was left after Saturday night worship. Thirty weeks into Lynne's employment, the personnel committee met with Jim to present a list of charges against Lynne, demanding her dismissal from the church staff. A mere seven months after Lynne's arrival, Jim was back in the position of leading Saturday night worship and was faced with an angry worshiping community who did not understand the sudden departure of a valued worship leader.

What happened? Jim wanted to be an empowering leader. He wanted to develop the people who worked with him, and he wanted to bring new people into positions of leadership. In fact, he knew it was essential for the growth, health, and well-being of the ministry at First Church. Jim had no interest in hanging on to power as head of staff. Yet over and over he experienced the same phenomenon that he had experienced with Lynne. The church did not seem willing to let someone new step into leadership. And the new people whom Jim tried to empower through delegation never seemed to lead in a way that reassured members of the congregation of their competence. Jim was beginning to believe that the congregation was run by a cantankerous group of old-timers who did not want to see change or welcome new leaders.

We can better understand what happened at First Church by turning to the work of Ken Blanchard, John Carlos, and Alan Randolph in *The Three Keys to Empowerment*. Blanchard describes the conditions needed to create an empowered work environment—an environment where willing and capable subordinates can be effectively developed for positions of shared leadership. The authors provide a structure for diagnosing and managing situations like the one Jim faced with Lynne and First Church. The model is known as Situational Leadership II.[3]

Situational Leadership II is based on creating a match between an individual's *development level* (various combinations of competence and commitment) on a specific goal or task and the *leadership style* (various combinations of directive and supportive behavior) the leader applies.

When assessing an individual's readiness to take on a new area of responsibility, Situational Leadership II requires paying attention to the development level of the employee, which is comprised of his or her competence and commitment level. *Competence* is the knowledge and skills an individual brings to a goal or task. Competence may be gained through formal education, on-the-job training, and experience. An employee's competence is best determined by demonstrated performance on the job.

The second component of an employee's development level is determined by his or her commitment. *Commitment* is a combination of an individual's motivation and self-confidence regarding a goal or task. Interest and enthusiasm are exhibited behaviorally through attentiveness, animation, energy levels, and facial expressions, as well as verbal cues. Confidence is characterized by a person's self-assuredness. If either motivation or confidence is low, commitment as a whole is considered low.[4]

In the First Church example, Lynne's developmental readiness could be assessed using the Situational Leadership II criteria. Jim had every reason to believe that Lynne was competent as a worship leader. She was hired for her skills in that area. Lynne, however, was new to First Church. Regardless of her skill in worship leadership, she could not have been fully competent in her role because she did not know the operating environment at First Church. Jim should have assumed a low level of competence until Lynne demonstrated otherwise. On the commitment level, Jim had every reason to believe that Lynne was committed. She was attentive in her work, highly animated, and approached her work with great energy. Jim's diagnosis of the initial situation, therefore, should have told him that Lynne was questionable, or low, in competence and high in commitment.

The combination of a staff member's competence level and commitment level determines the type of leadership style you apply as you seek to empower the employee. The leadership style you choose will be characterized by a combination of *supportive* behaviors and *directive* behaviors. Directive behaviors concentrate on how to do a task-telling and showing people what to do and when to do it and providing frequent feedback on results. Directive behaviors build competence in your staff member. Supportive behaviors focus on developing initiative and on the attitudes and feelings toward the task. Supportive behaviors might include praising, listening, encouraging, and involving. Support is instrumental in building commitment in others. The Situational Leadership II model proposes four basic leadership styles in which you match the staff member's commitment and competence level with your supportive and directive behaviors:

- *Style 1—Directing.* Your style combines high directive behaviors and low supportive behaviors. This style is directed at the staff member who has a low level of competence but a high level of commitment.

- *Style 2—Coaching.* Your style combines high directive behaviors with high supportive behaviors. This style is used with the staff member who has lower levels of competence and low commitment.
- *Style 3—Supporting.* Your style combines high supportive behaviors with low directive behaviors. This style is used with the staff member who has moderate to high competence levels and variable levels of commitment.
- *Style 4—Delegating.* Your style combines low supportive behaviors and low directive behaviors. This style is used with the staff member who has a high level of competence and a high level of commitment.

Returning to the case at First Church, the Situational Leadership II model can shed light on Jim's leadership relationship with Lynne. We already have determined that Lynne was high in commitment and low in competence when she arrived at First Church. But Jim was relieved at her arrival. He was eager to relinquish his responsibilities with the Saturday night worshiping community. Jim chose a delegating leadership style, using leadership behaviors that were nondirective and nonsupporting. He left Lynne alone to do her own thing. As a result, Lynne floundered. Whatever level of experience Lynne may have had in worship leadership, she was not experienced at First Church. She did not know the ins and outs of negotiating her way through this new system of people and processes, and she needed leadership behaviors from Jim that were more directive. Had Jim spent more directive time with Lynne in her early days at First Church, she might still be on staff and he might not be back leading Saturday night worship. Within a short period of time, Jim could have developed Lynn into a fully competent worship leader.

In the early stages, Jim could have stayed involved with Saturday night leadership and the decision making around that service to help Lynne understand more about life at First Church. In all likelihood, as Lynne learned more about her new assignment, some of her initial enthusiasm and commitment may have waned. Jim could have used a supportive coaching leadership style during that period until Lynne's competence began to grow. An increase in her competence level would have prompted less directive behavior from Jim and more encouragement and support. Finally, when Lynne's competence and confidence were both well established, Jim could have chosen a more delegating style. Jim's decision to move directly into a delegating style of management cost him and First Church the time and expense of a failed staff relationship.

In the Gospels of Matthew, Mark, and Luke, we encounter Jesus sending his twelve disciples out to do ministry in pairs of two—to continue and expand the work he began. Jesus did not send them forth because he was fed up and wanted someone else to pick up the ball. He sent them forth because the need was great and there was only so much of Jesus to go around. He sent them forth because they were ready, having sat at Jesus's feet and studied his teachings. Looking at this example, we can see that Jesus did four critical things to establish a healthy delegation relationship with his disciples:

1. He gave them power and authority. They didn't have to do the work as disempowered workers. Jesus shared his authority as teacher and healer with them. He proclaimed their power and authority.

2. He provided them with specific responsibility—directions about where they were to go, what they were to do and say, and where they were to stay.

3. He provided them with support. He sent them out in pairs so they didn't have to operate in an isolated or abandoned state.

4. He anticipated and accepted failure, telling them what they were to do in the event they were not welcomed or their teaching was not received. He provided direction for how they were to recover and move on.

The Key to Effective Delegation

Effective delegation comes down to creating a proper balance among three critical organizational elements:

Figure 7.1

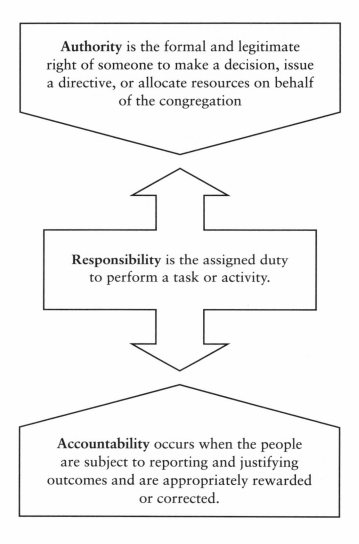

Delegation is effective when a person who is given responsibility for the performance of a task is also given an appropriate level of authority to execute the task and is held appropriately accountable for outcomes. The delegation relationship will go wrong if you do any of the following:

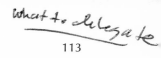

- *Fail to assign enough authority*. The person may try to do the task and fail because the organization will not give him or her the latitude to do what you have asked.
- *Assign too much authority*. Too much authority too soon may lead the person to become heavy-handed and take responsibility for things that you did not want her or him to do.
- *Fail to define responsibility*. When individuals are not clear about what you have asked them to do, they will invent their own boundaries around the task.
- *Fail to maintain accountability*. The person may fail to do the task because there are no consequences for nonperformance. Or, worse yet, the person may perform the task successfully but then become discouraged and withdrawn because there was no recognition for a job well done.

What to Delegate

The senior leader may have determined that a staff member is ready for a delegating style of leadership. The leader still needs to make appropriate choices about what to delegate. Delegating the wrong tasks can be just as detrimental as delegating to people who are not ready for a delegating style of leadership. What are the "right" kinds of tasks to delegate?

- *Tasks that can be done better by someone else.* Every staff member has some area of giftedness, some particular gift in ministry. Choices about what to delegate should be grounded in the spiritual giftedness of the staff person. Delegate those responsibilities that others are naturally better at doing. They may be better at the task by virtue of raw talent, education or training, or temperament.
- *Tasks that are time critical but not a high priority*. A painter may be waiting in the church office for instructions on how to lay out the lines in the church parking lot. His presence in the office makes the decision time critical; he is paid by

the hour to be at the church. The urgency of the situation, however, should not automatically make the task a high priority for the senior leader. Delegate the task to someone else who is prepared to handle the urgency of the situation and for whom the task is appropriate.

- *Tasks of appropriate difficulty.* The person to whom work is delegated should feel challenged but not overwhelmed. A good benchmark is to craft the task so that learning mistakes are likely to occur but self-confidence and/or reputation are not destroyed. For example, the senior minister might allow a new choir director to select hymns for worship. He delegates this task even though he is aware that some of the choir director's favorites are considered distasteful to members of this congregation. The senior minister knows that the choir director is going to receive negative feedback, so he cautions her and decides to let her make those choices anyway as part of a growth process for both the employee and the congregation. The same senior minister may not delegate the selection of hymns for the Mother's Day service or on Christmas Eve when people are less likely to be gracious about unpopular musical choices.

- *Both pleasant and unpleasant tasks.* Some tasks are unpleasant for everyone. Not many people consider the making of coffee or the taking out of garbage as a growth experience. Unpleasant tasks should be rotated fairly among all staff members. Heads of staff should keep a portion of unpleasant tasks for themselves to demonstrate a willingness to serve the members of their staff.

- *Tasks that are not central to the role of the senior pastor.* Some tasks are symbolically important or politically sensitive and need to be handled by the senior pastor, even though they are not technically difficult tasks to perform. Senior leaders should never delegate a task that is central to their role. For example, an important dignitary in the community visits the church to learn more about one of the social ministry programs. The senior pastor may determine that another member of the staff actually knows more about this ministry and should be the focal point of the dignitary's visit. This, however, will not excuse the senior pastor from meeting with the dignitary as a sign of respect. The role as head of staff has a figurehead component that must be honored, regardless of how you delegate the components of a task.

How to Delegate

Planning to Delegate

Once the senior leader determines that a staff member is ready for a delegating style of leadership and an appropriate task has been identified, the leader needs to prepare for delegation in several important ways.

Plan to spend enough time with the person on the delegated task. At the beginning it is common for people to take much longer than expected to complete a task. This is because the person to whom work is delegated is still learning how to do the work. During this stage it may occur to the leader that she could have done the work more quickly herself. Be patient and persistent! The investment of time and energy will pay off in the long run.

Determine what level of authority is to be assigned along with the task. Also define the limits of discretion. Consider the following layers of authority:

Stage 1. You gather the facts; I will make the decision.
Stage 2. Give me some options for how to proceed; I still decide.
Stage 3. Make a recommendation to me; I continue to decide.
Stage 4. You decide; I approve.
Stage 5. Make your decision, inform me, and act upon it unless I say no.
Stage 6. You do it and tell me about it.
Stage 7. Do it, and advise me only if you are unsuccessful.
Stage 8. You take care of it; leave me out of it.

Bear in mind that the leader can never delegate more authority than the leader possesses. Even the senior pastor's position in the congregation has limits attached to it. Senior clergy are empowered to make certain kinds of decisions and to use certain types of resources. When delegating to a member of the staff, the leader can never give him or her more decision-making authority than the leader holds herself. Be careful not to fall into the trap of delegating tasks that are unwanted because of the leader's own limited access to resources. If the leader cannot get the task done because of lack of authority, a staff member will have even less success. The senior minister who is frustrated that the choir director won't consider his suggestions for special music can't try and delegate that task to another member of the staff team.

When the leader assigns a delegated task, there are a variety of steps to be followed to ensure that the process of delegation flows smoothly:

Assigning the Task

1. Explain the purpose of the job so that the person to whom you are delegating the task understands the big picture and how this task fits into it.
2. Specify responsibilities clearly. Explain expected results, objectives, priorities, and deadlines that must be met. Check for comprehension.
3. Specify the level of authority that you have decided to assign. Explain the limits of discretion, including funds that can be committed, resources that can be used, decisions that can be made without approval, and agreements that can be negotiated directly with those outside the congregation.
4. Specify reporting requirements. Clarify the types of information that you expect to receive back on the progress of the task, the manner in which progress is to be monitored (i.e., written reports, face-to-face meetings, staff meetings), and the frequency and timing of progress reviews. More frequent checking is appropriate for critical tasks

with high exposure and high cost of mistakes and for staff members who lack experience and confidence. As the person demonstrates greater competence in doing delegated tasks, the frequency of reporting should be reduced.

5. Ensure acceptance of responsibilities. Have the employee or volunteer describe back to you, in his or her own words, what has been decided upon. This helps to clarify what the employee thinks he or she has agreed to do and what level of responsibility he or she is prepared to accept.[5]

Monitoring the Assignment

1. Inform others who need to know. People who are affected by the delegation and people whose cooperation and assistance are necessary to do the delegated tasks should be informed about the newly assigned responsibilities and authority. Note that the person to whom you are delegating cannot establish his or her own authority. You must do it for that person.

2. Arrange for the staff member or volunteer to receive necessary information on a timely basis. It usually is best to have all detailed information about the task flow directly to the person rather than through you. Make sure that you keep the person informed about any changes in the life of the congregation that may affect his or her plans and schedules.

3. Monitor progress at appropriate, agreed-upon intervals. Check in with the employee or volunteer at the times that were agreed upon when the task was assigned. More frequent check-ins will make the person feel that he or she is being policed. Less frequent check-ins will generate feelings of abandonment.

4. Be available to provide coaching and answer questions where appropriate.

5. Accept the fact that there is more than one way to get at any given problem. Allow the person latitude in her or his

choice of how to proceed. Do not demand that he or she
do it just the way you would have.

6. Be mindful that you can never fully delegate all of the
    responsibility associated with a task. When you delegate,
    you always bear some level of responsibility for comple-
    tion of the task.

Handling Results

1. Only receive high-quality work. When a job is delivered
    back to you, allow enough time to check it thoroughly. If
    you accept partly completed work, you will have to invest
    time in completing it, and the person to whom you have
    delegated will not have learned to do the work to the
    required standard.

2. Provide support and encouragement, but avoid reverse
    delegation. Make certain that you redirect and bolster a
    project that is going astray. Do not take back responsibil-
    ity for a task that already was delegated. If you are asked
    to provide help, ask the person to present you with a rec-
    ommended solution for his or her own problem. You can
    evaluate whether or not the solution is feasible without
    taking back responsibility for the larger task.

3. Make mistakes a learning experience. When you delegate,
    mistakes are inevitable. Treat failures seriously, but avoid
    shaming or blaming. In an open and encouraging manner,
    discuss the mistakes and identify ways to avoid similar
    mistakes in the future.

4. If appropriate, reward the effort. If someone has done
    good work for you, let that person know. Appropriate
    praise will help to build confidence and efficiency the next
    time he or she does a task for you. When rewarding a
    positive outcome, praise delivered in a public setting will
    always be more effective than praise delivered privately.

Earlier in this text (chapter 1) we spoke against the notion of head
of staff as the "genius with a thousand helpers." Effective staff

teams in thriving congregations have mastered the art of delegation in such a way that empowerment replaces the role of a singular genius. Careful attention to the basics of planning to delegate, assigning the task, monitoring the assignment, and handling results will insure an empowered and aligned staff team.

Chapter 8

Helping Staff Negotiate Their Needs

Senior clergy, personnel committees, and others who share supervisory roles are responsible to bring order and structure to work so that people can be productive. This book provides a number of ways to support that need for order and structure. On the individual level, personnel committees and senior clergy pay attention to developing job descriptions, clarifying expectations and outcomes for the work of each staff person, and developing practices of performance management. On the group level, senior clergy lead staff meetings, pay attention to group development issues, develop paths of communication and information sharing, and provide opportunities for personal sharing, spiritual deepening, and social engagement. At the level of work flow, agreements are made and norms are established so that people know what to expect of one another. Everyone knows that information for the church newsletter has to be given to the communications staff person two weeks in advance. An "on-call" schedule is posted in the church office so that everyone knows who is to pick up emergency and random calls while others have the day off.

But it is the nature of things to change. Just when we get everything organized, it all begins to unravel. Policies and practices are in place. Standards and agreements have been set. Yet discomfort within an individual or within the larger staff appears, and all that seemed to work now begins to hit a bump or two. Those of us who like the really "big picture" explanations can blame the second law of thermodynamics and the principle of entropy, which states that everything moves with a tendency toward disorder. It can be comforting to know that the whole universe has a way of winding down and losing order. But more realistically for the staff of a congregation, the truth is that it is simply the nature of things to change. As a person or team's work develops, people must meet new challenges that require changes in order to respond. While people naturally try to accommodate the group, the longer one is in a job or a relationship, the more one's personal preferences and styles begin to kick in—often to the surprise of others. This chapter will provide models with which to understand and negotiate such changes.

It is helpful for leaders to understand fundamental principles of group development that play a large role in the instability of the people and groups we are trying to lead.[1] Groups start out in a stage of politeness in which people test if they, in fact, can join and really belong to the group. Staff members are polite to one another and work to find ways in which they are the same or can appear the same. The addition of a new staff person typically invites the whole group to revert to this stage of politeness and formation. Once the members feel that they belong, however, the stage of politeness moves to a stage of testing in which people behave according to their own preferences to see if the group will accommodate them. While this stage of group life still may be approached professionally and even graciously, it is nonetheless a time of discomfort in which what was expected now somehow has changed to the surprise of others. By testing and negotiating these personal differences and preferences, the group enters into the more mature stage of making agreements (setting norms) for their work together, which allows them to become productive. Every time a new staff member joins the team and every time the nature or requirements of the team's work changes, however, the group development cycle kicks in again.

There is no reason to despair here. This is simply the nature of group life and interpersonal relationships. The normal steps of group development are the way in which people build trust and confidence in one another and are the path to real productivity. Progressing through these steps, however, does carry the reminder that as hard as we work as senior leaders to bring order and structure to the people and the work of our staff, the reality is that constant negotiation of expectations and needs is fundamental to the life of any group.

Staff Need Help to Negotiate Changes

When people do not negotiate their differences, the conflict tends to lead either to a blowup or to icy silence. Whenever we receive a threatening message, such as something unexpected or not agreed upon, the information is carried to and managed by the part of our brain that is designed to respond to threats.[2] This is the least evolved part of our brain—often called the reptilian core. It has few feelings and little reason. Nevertheless, it does manage the two primary ways of dealing with threats—fight and flight.

In fight we move aggressively toward the threat; in flight we move protectively away from the threat. While working with congregations, both Susan and Gil have been in any number of staff meetings in which a staff member responds unexpectedly—perhaps even surprising himself or herself—with a statement that begins something like this: "There is no way I am going to do that!" One staff with which Gil worked had a member who blew up quite frequently but did it ever so graciously. He simply would register his surprise or dismay by exclaiming, "Oh, my stars!" This is a quiet "blowup" to be sure, but people knew something was not right for this staff member. The fight response does not necessarily mean a confrontation. It does, however, signal a discomfort that the person wants to engage.

In flight people move away from their discomfort—either into personal silence or protected space. Think of the times you have witnessed yourself or others say nothing in a staff meeting but quickly pick up the subject after the meeting in a trusted coworker's office with the door closed.

While in the long run both the fight and flight responses are unhelpful in identifying and resolving the surprise or discomfort experienced in the group, we need to recognize them as normal and natural behaviors for all people—all species as a matter of fact.

While these behaviors may not be the most helpful to resolve the issue, they certainly are signals that there are issues that need to be resolved. Staff, like all groups, typically need help in doing this work of resolution.

A Model for Understanding the Dynamics of Relational Negotiation

John Sherwood and John Scherer, organizational consultants and counselors, have developed a helpful model of planned renegotiation, which has direct application both for marriage (negotiation between two people) and for staff teams (negotiation among a number of people).[3] They identify shared information as the key to building a relationship and to negotiating changes in that relationship: "What building a relationship means is exchanging sufficient information so that the behavior of both parties is more or less predictable, and uncertainty is reduced to an acceptable level."[4] A model of a developing relationship, complete with the normative bumps that will be experienced and the opportunities for negotiation, can be seen in the figure below:

Figure 8.1

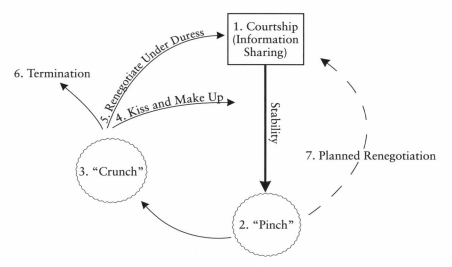

It is perhaps easiest to walk through this model using the experience of a hypothetical couple recently married and navigating the common bumps and discomforts of living together. The parallels to the life and development of all pairs and groups are transparent. Let us walk through the stages:

1. *The courtship stage.* This is the initial coming together of the two people when it is clear that the relationship is important and that it is worth investing in. To deepen the relationship, the individuals share information about themselves so that the other can know what to expect. She learns that he loves to read and that he would much rather read the book before seeing the movie and not vice versa. He learns that she values punctuality and will even tell him that a party starts a half hour earlier than it actually does so that he will be on time.

Through the sharing of information, both intentional and unintentional, each will develop trustworthy expectations of the other that provide role clarity for each in the newly developing relationship. They feel that they know what to expect and how to behave in the relationship. This initial sharing of information provides a good bit of stability to the relationship so that the couple can set off on their path together, moving toward and through the wedding and into a marriage relationship that they can enjoy. After the wedding they assume all is well and feel that they know what is needed to make the marriage "work." The polite stage of knowing that they "belong" together has been managed. It is time to settle in and get started.

2. *The "pinch."* All goes well, and stability is, in fact, experienced because the information the couple shared in the courtship stage provided role clarity and commitment. The dilemma is that we never can share all the needed information that will address every situation and the many changes that will need to be faced. It also is important to note that in the courtship stage—the beginning of any relationship—we do not consciously choose to share all information about ourselves, but tend more readily to share the positive side—putting our "best foot forward." The limitation of the politeness of the initial stage of formation is an overfocus on the positive things most easily shared. There still are unknowns to

be discovered and surprises to encounter. These discoveries and surprises are often encountered as "pinches."

A "pinch" is the first dawning awareness that something is not quite right or that something feels a bit amiss. A pinch is rarely perceived as a *problem* at the beginning, but it rather is experienced as a *discomfort*. While the pinch is actually a choice point that offers an opportunity to deepen the relationship by sharing more information, the greater tendency is to gloss over the discomfort. Sherwood and Scherer are clear in their assumption that there are actually pressures not to respond to pinches.[5] Culturally we are not encouraged to listen to our own feelings, so pinches might go unnoticed. Even when they are noticed, we are trained not to share them. We are taught to "get along by going along."

In the case of our young married couple, the pinch might be the trash that is piling up in the kitchen. Assuming stereotypical gender roles for the moment, let us say that the young wife is in the kitchen cooking and notices that the trash can is full, so she asks her new husband to empty the can, which he willingly does. All is well. Two days later, however, she sees that the can is full again. She asks him to empty it again, which he does, and all is still well. But two days later the can is full and again he has done nothing about it. She must ask again. He complies, but suddenly it feels a bit different. *Why isn't he helping out around the house?* she asks herself. *Why is she always nagging me about trash?* he wonders. The pinch is felt, but it is not a big issue, so the young couple continue on by dismissing the discomfort. As we will see, the ability to recognize and respond to pinches as they are experienced is a mark of health and maturity. Our cultural nature, however, is not to attend to these pinches right away. So let's move on to the next stage in the model.

3. *The "crunch."* Crunches come from unresolved pinches. Pinches that are not addressed continue and finally are perceived as a violation of an expectation or a trust. A crunch is a series or history of pinches that now seem worth fighting over. The behavior that was once a nuisance now easily can be seen as a bellwether for the relationship itself. She no longer just wonders why he is not helping. She now begins to ask herself, *Why doesn't he love me anymore?* He has moved from wondering about nagging to wishing

she would leave him alone. The pinch, once matured into a crunch, now intrudes on the relationship. This quite often prompts a "fight" or "flight"—a disruption in the relationship.

As shown in figure 8.1, once the crunch is experienced, the young couple have a number of choices about how to respond.

4. *"Kissing and making up."* A very typical response is to "kiss and make up." Somewhere in the fight—the disruption in the relationship—the couple pause and remember what they are trying to do in the marriage. "Wait," one of them will say. "This is foolish. Why are we arguing about trash?" They will reconsider what is important to them; they will recall their love for one another; they will recognize that trash is not really important; and they will suggest to each other that they "kiss and make up." After all, they really do love each other.

People who find great meaning and purpose in their work respond in very much the same way. When experiencing discomfort that leads to a disruption, we commonly remind ourselves and others of the bigger purpose of our mission and dismiss both the fight or flight and the unmet expectation or repeated surprise that caused the disturbance. After all, we say, this is really about "God" or "the body of Christ" or "the mission of the congregation."

The critical issue about kissing and making up is that *nothing is changed*. The young married couple—or the coworkers on a staff—reaffirm their initial purpose and relationship and seek to go back to the way it was before they encountered the pinch. And so they do. Feeling better, they pick up where they left off, and all is well again.

And two days later the trash can is full. She stews. He doesn't move.

Sherwood and Scherer point out that pinches that are unresolved lead with increased frequency to crunches of increased intensity.[6] Unaddressed, there is less time between the pinches and the crunches, more time spent in the crunch stage, and greater damage to the relationship.

5. *Renegotiation under duress.* Another choice that the young couple might make is to renegotiate their experience and relationship under duress. Because they have been fighting about the trash,

they might be both bruised and puzzled by why something so trivial would set them against one another, and so they decide to seek help. Going to their pastor, they say that they have been fighting over trivial things and need help. The pastor begins to talk with them and ask questions about what has been going on. It is important to note that this renegotiation under duress is another time of learning. More information is solicited and shared about expectations and preferences. Under duress the additional information often needs to be solicited by a third party who has responsibility to promote a safe environment in which the people may talk openly. Information that was missing from the courtship stage may now be added. New learning with new information has the potential of reestablishing a new stability in the relationship.

Trying to be helpful, the pastor inquires about families of origin. When he asks the young wife who used to take out the trash when she was growing up, she answers quickly, "Why, my dad, of course. And he never needed to be asked." Turning to the young husband, the pastor asks the same question about who took out the trash when he was growing up. Puzzled, he answers, "I don't know. It just kind of disappeared. I never thought about it."

By uncovering new information, the pastor helps the young couple understand and renegotiate their expectations of one another. They revisit the same kind of information sharing that occurred in their courtship and originally provided the safe and steady expectations that they enjoyed in the earliest stages of their relationship. As can be seen in figure 8.1, the steady stage after information sharing and negotiation of expectations never continues uninterrupted. It inevitably leads to the next step and stages of pinches, which also will need to be negotiated. Disruption is inevitable. The information that we have about one another is always incomplete. The circumstances in which we live—and work—are always changing.

6. *Termination.* A third option that the young couple have after experiencing their multiple rounds of pinch-crunch-pinch-crunch is to move toward termination. Unaddressed and unresolved, the normal and natural disruptions in expectations create pain and a divide that can become too large for people to want to bridge. Rec-

ognizing that they do not trust their expectations of one another, that they are hurt and are hurting the other, and that they cannot seem to stop, the couple may move toward separation and divorce.

7. *Planned renegotiation.* The critical insight of Sherwood and Scherer's model is that an often unrecognized option available to the young couple is planned renegotiation, which happens when a pinch is first recognized. After the second or third round of the trash can's filling up and only the young wife noticing it, it is much healthier for the couple to identify the experience, laugh a bit about it, and then ask, "What's going on here?"

We already have acknowledged that this is not a typical or normal response since we are trained not to identify or confront such bumps in our relationships. Sherwood and Scherer, however, say that when people understand the natural development of all relationships as described in this model, there is both reason and language to talk about pinches in a timely way that can make a difference. The couple still may want to visit their pastor in order to have the help and safety of talking about their experience with someone. The relationship, however, is not damaged, unmet expectations have not become relationship problems, and the couple are working at building the relationship as opposed to repairing the relationship.

We hope the parallel between the developing relationship of a young couple through courtship and into marriage and the developing relationship of staff teams is an easy jump for the reader to make. The job descriptions, outcomes, staff meetings, and other tools and practices put in place provide the fundamental information sharing (courtship) that allows team members to set off on a relatively secure path with clear expectations. The reality, however, is that no matter how complete leaders try to be with information and expectations, it is not possible to negotiate everything at the beginning. Time and change introduce new needs, making the ongoing renegotiation of relationships necessary. Staff members will need to renegotiate their expectations, assumptions, and relationships because of the inevitable pinches that will always lie ahead. Failing to negotiate the pinches leads to crunches, which commonly are experienced as major distractions from ministry. Renegotiation at the pinch points, however, is not natural. Staff need help to do this.

Staff Need Help Knowing What to Negotiate

Pinches are "small" discomforts that tend not to be negotiated by staff members, because as "team players," it feels inappropriate to complain. Staff members want good relationships and an enjoyable working environment and are reluctant to risk these on small matters. It is not easy to see how small matters naturally can escalate into crunches, so staff members tend to accommodate. Examples of disruptions in expectations to which colleagues typically respond with initial accommodation include the following:

- the colleague who sets a time to meet but is habitually late himself
- the colleague who goes into someone's office and sits to talk leisurely, seemingly unaware that the other person is busy
- the colleague who tells a third party information about someone's work without talking with that person first
- the colleague who is on a list of e-mail chatter (i.e., jokes, stories, puzzles) and forwards them to everyone else
- the colleague who waits for the public moment of a staff meeting to share information with a team member that should have been shared privately
- the colleague who disagrees with a decision publicly after the meeting is over

Such accommodations feel like minor issues, and we could not hope to renegotiate all of them all the time. There is a need for give-and-take in all relationships that prize the relationship over perfection. But because these accommodations feel like small and inconsequential concessions, staff do not feel the freedom to address the small uncomfortable pinches when they are barriers to work and to healthy team relationships. Staff need permission and guidance from the senior leader to address these issues in responsible ways.

When working with staff on issues of team development, it is common for consultants to offer examples such as those above. Being able to see the kind of natural disruptions that we all experience encourages staff members and allows them to legitimize their feelings about these smaller behaviors that, while commonly minimized, are significant barriers to productivity and our work together.

Staff Need Help Knowing How to Negotiate

Planned renegotiation is a structured conversation that has both guidelines and boundaries to make it safe. It is rarely helpful simply to invite people to disclose anything and everything that bothers them about the people with whom they work or about their own job. It is more likely that honesty will prevail and change will be the result when people are given some structure for the conversation and feel safe to participate. The leader is responsible to provide such safe space and direction, which Ronald Heifetz, cofounder of Harvard University's Center for Public Leadership, refers to as a "holding environment."[7] Like a therapist who uses the limited time and the privacy of the therapeutic hour to provide safety that encourages the client to speak openly, the staff leader must provide a holding environment in which it is safe for staff members to renegotiate their needs with one another.

Two Models of Role Renegotiation

Staff Meetings

It is appropriate occasionally to place "issues of our life and work together" on the agenda for a regular staff meeting. Such a conversation may be limited to a fifteen- to twenty-minute segment of the meeting and can be given both safety and structure by providing guidelines. The first step is to state clearly the issue or the part of staff work and life that is to be discussed. Examples might include the following:

- The way we share information. Do we all get what we need or too much or too little?
- The way we make decisions. Do we know when we have made decisions and how we do it?
- Our life together. Do we experience behaviors in our relationships with other staff members that make it more difficult for us to do our work?

The senior clergy can shape an agenda question that will direct staff members to the conversation that would be most helpful for them to have. The staff members are then invited into the conversation, following very clear guidelines, such as the following:

- We will stick to the topic. While we might look at other issues of our work together at another time, for this conversation we will focus our comments and observations on the identified topic.
- We will speak only from our own experience and not try to speak on behalf of others or use hearsay information.
- We will be specific in using examples that will help others understand and not generalize.
- Just because we say it, does not mean other people have to do it.

Following the structured conversation, the staff may then be asked to reflect on what they have heard, using two additional questions:

1. What do we hear in our conversation that would improve our life and our work together?
2. What conversations (between whom) need to continue on this issue following this staff meeting?

The reflection questions can be addressed within a few minutes to bring closure to this agenda item and to identify any next steps that should be followed.

Staff Team Retreat

Team Retreats

Reviewing and renegotiating working relationships is appropriate for retreat time with staff members. By retreat we mean anything from a full morning to a several-day experience in which the team meets off-site with the specific intent of looking at their work and life together. When afforded the luxury of such time, several hours can be given to a role renegotiation exercise that invites team members to be intentional in their feedback and requests of their coworkers. The exercise might include the following segments:

Introduction to role renegotiation. The leader can rehearse the Sherwood-Scherer model outlined above, using an example such as the young married couple's negotiation of taking out the trash. Using a simple and understandable example like this gives people clear insight into the dynamics of group development but also models the very natural need to negotiate the "smaller" issues that too easily tend to be glossed over.

Examples from "life." Team members are then invited into a very brief brainstorming of the renegotiation issues that they can identify in their own experiences with family and friends. It also can be helpful to invite people to think of and share examples from movies, television, or literature. By beginning the conversation with examples from "outside" their own group of colleagues, there is recognition of the commonness and naturalness of the need for role renegotiation that provides a sense of safety later— when members will be asked to think about their own work with their colleagues. As in all such interpersonal exercises, laughter and a sense of play are important and bring more safety to the conversation.

Identifying our own experience. Staff members then will be invited to do some personal reflection on their own, thinking about what they need from others to be more productive and to become a better team member in ministry. Each person will be given the following handout to make personal notes for his or her own use.

Role Renegotiation Exercise

In the spaces below, write down what you want each of the other members of your staff to do less of or more of and what you want them to keep doing the same. Please be specific, and focus on *actual behavior* (not personality or attitude).

Name of Colleague	Do Less of	Do More of	Keep Doing the Same

This sheet is for your own thinking. You will not be asked to share it with any person or hand it in later. The purpose for filling out this sheet is to help you be clear about what you hope to negotiate. For example, "I need you to refer parishioner complaints directly to me" or "I would like you to limit the copies of e-mails you send to people with whom we work and not send everything, including your thank-yous and confirmations of their e-mails." Remember that simply because you ask for some change, you cannot assume that it will be made. The goal is to negotiate what behaviors will work best for both you and the other person.

Working individually, staff members are invited to fill in the columns on the worksheet for every colleague whose name is listed in the left-hand column. For a large staff in which every staff person does not work directly with everyone else, it may be more helpful to break the team into working units so that each staff member is filling out the worksheet only for the persons with whom they have a direct working relationship.

Sharing our needs. After people have done their individual work, they are invited back to the larger group for sharing. The invitation is for each staff person to take a turn addressing colleagues individually using the worksheet they have prepared. Remind people that the worksheet is a private document and that they do not need to read everything written on it if they choose not to. The opportunity is to say what would be helpful to each person with whom they work.

Note: It is important for the most senior member of the team to go first in this part of the exercise. The senior member can model the kind of sharing that is helpful as well as model attention to negotiating *behaviors* and not *personalities.* Be careful not to put staff members in a position in which they might be embarrassed by going first and sharing more openly or honestly than the person who supervises them is willing to do.

Each staff person is invited to take time in the full group to address each of the coworkers on the left-hand column of their worksheet individually by talking about what they need less of, more of, or the same of from that person. The responsibility of the person being addressed is to listen and at the end of the feedback to respond briefly to three questions:

1. What did I hear?
2. What do I know that I can do or cannot do in response to this information?
3. What do you (the presenter of the feedback) and I need to talk about more at another time to figure out what we can do?

The nature of things—such as our work and our working relationships—is to change. Negotiating that inevitable change and renegotiating our working relationships with one another are critical to the path of both productivity and faithfulness.

Chapter 9

Performance Evaluation

Building on Strength

Steve sat in his office, stunned and dismayed by the experience he had just been through. For the past six weeks he had dreaded delivering this performance review, and the events that transpired certainly fulfilled all of his worst expectations. The review meeting ended with Diane calling him a liar, storming out of the office, and threatening to place a call to their district superintendent. Looking back over the review meeting, Steve knew exactly when things began to go wrong: it was when he started talking with Diane about how she managed her personal relationships in the congregation. In retrospect he still could not figure out what he should have done differently. As things now stood, Diane still was not taking any ownership of her problem with boundary setting, and the relationship between the two of them seemed irretrievably broken.

Diane was a dynamic minister of music and excelled in worship leadership. Her extreme extroversion allowed her to connect quickly and easily with people in a worship context, and her musical talents were considerable. Everyone who knew Diane from a distance loved her. But Diane had some problems in one-on-one relationships. In the early stages of a relationship, people responded well to her. Inevitably, Diane overinvested herself in the lives of congregants. She did not make distinctions between friendship and ministry relationships. Most painfully for Steve, she often used those "boundaryless" relationships to undermine Steve's reputation in the congregation. Here's an example of how the scenario would unfold: Someone who had received a pastoral care visit with the arrival of a new baby suddenly became Diane's new best friend. Diane could be found at the young couple's house for dinner on a regular basis. Then Steve would begin feeling himself alienated from the young couple, and stories would leak out into the congregation, through the couple, about things that had happened between Steve and Diane in a staff meeting. This pattern had repeated itself on at least three different occasions. Diane would grow closer and closer to her new best friends, then suddenly the relationship would end and she would move on to a new relationship.

Now as Steve pondered the outcome of his meeting with Diane, he was at a loss about where he should go from here.

In January 2002 the Alban Institute conducted an informal e-mail survey to ask congregational leaders how frequently they were evaluated on their performance and how helpful they found that evaluation. Sixty-five percent of respondents indicated that their performance was reviewed annually. Almost half of the respondents indicated that their personal evaluation process was either "a little" or "not at all" helpful to their development as a leader.[1]

Frankly, most of us would rather visit the dentist for a root canal than sit down in a one-on-one conversation about performance. A corporate mind-set embraces the notion that you need to measure performance if you want to improve it and that you have to high-light weaknesses if you want people to address those weaknesses. This approach to performance management has worked itself into the culture of many of our congregations.

Why are we not doing better? Why do most church leaders utter a collective groan when faced with the topic of performance evaluation? Why do we have so many stories to tell of performance evaluation gone bad?

Why Performance Evaluation Fails

There are countless reasons why a performance appraisal meeting may go badly. Two particular problems, however, emerge over and over again in congregational settings, seeming to contribute to our unease with performance evaluations.

Performance evaluation often fails because we do not distinguish between problems related to the staff member (skills, abilities, and motivation) and problems related to the system or work environment that the staff member engages. Employees feel blamed for circumstances outside of their control and consequently reject all of the feedback rather than taking responsibility for the aspect of the problem that belongs to them.

In the early 1980s, W. Edwards Deming began to question the wisdom in measuring and evaluating performance. Deming generally is recognized as the philosopher-guru of the Total Quality movement in manufacturing environments. In his seminal work *Out of the Crisis*, Deming cited "seven deadly diseases of management." One of the deadly diseases that Deming attacked was the personal evaluation of performance, including merit ratings, annual reviews, and management by objectives. According to Deming, the essential problem with most performance review systems is that they reward results rather than improvement, and that results almost always include an element of system luck. Too many supervisors hound people to try harder when the cause of mistakes is not worker attitude or effort, but rather the system within which the workers are stuck. Deming went so far as to suggest that 94 percent of commonly occurring performance problems are related to the system and only 6 percent of performance-related problems can be attributed to the action of the people performing the task.[2]

Behavioral scientist Geary Rummler has suggested that there are actually five factors in any given work situation that contribute to underlying performance problems. Most performance evaluation tends to lump problems in all five areas under a single category of flawed performance, which then is attributed entirely to the employee being evaluated. Only two of the five categories, in fact, pertain to things that the individual being evaluated can control. Rummler's five factors include the following:

- job situation—equipment, resources, or environment in which the work takes place

- individual performance—physical and emotional capacity and motivation to perform the required tasks
- response (action or decision by performer)—application of necessary skills, tools, or other resources
- consequences of action or decision to performer—logical and natural consequences for performing or not performing the task
- feedback—regular feedback of information about the value of performance

A second reason that performance evaluation regularly fails is that it tends to focus on the shortcomings of the individual rather than build upon the employee's strengths. Behavioral science increasingly is coming to understand that leaders cannot focus on the negative in employee performance and expect positive changes in behavior.

Earlier in this resource we referred to the work of Marcus Buckingham and the research project conducted for the Gallup Organization to identify the core strengths of truly great managers. Buckingham reflects further upon his learnings in *The One Thing You Need to Know: . . . About Great Managing, Great Leading, and Sustained Individual Success*. During his research Buckingham attempted to answer the question "What are the things you need to know about a person to manage him or her effectively?" His research suggested a key distinction between what mediocre managers believe and what great managers believe:

> The mediocre manager believes that most things are learnable and therefore that the essence of management is to identify each person's weaker areas and eradicate them. The great manager believes the opposite. He [or she] believes that the most influential qualities of a person are innate, and therefore the essence of management is to deploy these innate qualities as effectively as possible and so drive performance.
>
> Current research suggests that accurate self-awareness rarely drives performance, and that in many circumstances, it actively

retards performance. Only self-assurance drives performance, even when this self-assurance turns out to be unrealistic.[3]

Relying on similar research, Donald Clifton and James Harter suggest that managers who use a strengths-based approach with their employees nearly double their likelihood of success in improving performance outcomes. Why does this occur? The belief is that people can change in certain areas of job performance—such as their satisfaction with the job, subjective well-being, engagement of the task, and performance—but they change best by working with their inherent talents, not by focusing on their weaknesses.[4]

Performance Evaluation: Why Bother?

Does this management research suggest that performance evaluation is doomed from the very start? Why should a congregation bother with it? Why not simply engage the quarterly performance planning meetings described in chapter 6 and let go of the annual evaluation?

Performance evaluation addresses a number of purposes, not all of which can be addressed in an abbreviated quarterly performance planning meeting. A performance evaluation that is done well, with an emphasis on building strengths, can accomplish several important organizational outcomes. Clinical psychologist and management consultant Harry Levinson suggests that performance appraisal and review has the ability to serve an organization in eight critical ways. He explains that performance evaluation:[5]

- Clarifies both the job to be done and the expectations of accomplishment. Job descriptions are not static. In chapter 4 we discussed the critical job description. During the annual review process, you are invited to acknowledge the ever-evolving roles of your staff members as they mature in their skills and grow in new directions. The annual performance review provides a forum for visiting job responsibilities and owning the variety of ways in which the ministry has evolved over the past year.

- <u>Measures and evaluates performance</u>. The performance appraisal that focuses on the strengths and talents of an employee still benefits from some level of measurement. On what core competencies has the employee been relying, over-relying, and/or underutilizing?
- <u>Serves as a basis for decisions about salary and promotion</u>. Much as leaders in congregations hate to grapple with this topic, they need to have some realistic and fair basis for the assignment of salary increases, promotions, and demotions. More will be said about the relationship between performance and pay at a later point in this chapter.
- <u>Serves as a device for organizational integration</u>. The six questions posed to the employee during the quarterly performance planning meeting are powerful questions that build upon strengths. Nevertheless, the senior staff member has to do some serious alignment of performance goals in the organization so that every staff member is not pursuing an individualized agenda. An annual comprehensive and standardized review process can build that alignment into the organization.

These first four objectives have a judgmental orientation because they focus on the past and provide a basis for making judgments regarding employee recognition. (See our discussion concerning summative and formative evaluations in chapter 6.) A judgmental orientation need not carry a negative connotation. We can judge past performance with an attitude of hope and from a place of strength.

The remaining four objectives cited by Levinson have more of a developmental focus because they are concerned with improving future performance by ensuring that expectations are clear and by identifying ways to facilitate employee performance through training and development. Those objectives are to:

- Relate individual performance to organizational goals.
- Foster the increasing competence and growth of the subordinate.

- Enhance communication between superior and subordinate.
- Stimulate the subordinate's motivation by clearly identifying and building upon strengths.

In addition to these secular arguments for establishing an annual review process, there are spiritual reasons to engage in annual evaluation. The annual review can be a powerful forum for discernment. Often people become aware of the movement of God in their lives only in retrospect. When staff reflect over the course of a year, they might identify God's leading hand in their ministry more clearly. Quarterly planning sessions may not provide a long enough perspective to evaluate how God is at work in the ministry of a congregation's staff. The annual performance review can provide senior clergy and their staff members with a prayerful, thoughtful forum for vocational discernment.

In *Evaluating Ministry: Principles and Processes for Clergy and Congregations*, Jill Hudson speaks about evaluation as one of God's ways of bringing the history of the past into dialogue with the hope for the future. She cites a wonderful quotation from a pamphlet prepared by the Division of Ordained Ministry of the United Methodist Church as a theological foundation for evaluation:[6]

Without confession of sin there is no reconciliation; without the counting of blessings there is no thanksgiving; without the acknowledgment of accomplishments there is no celebration; without awareness of potential there is no hope; without hope there is no desire for growth; and without a desire for growth the past will dwarf the future. We are called into new growth and new ministries by taking a realistic and hopeful look at what we have been and what we can still become. Surrounded by God's grace and the crowd of witnesses in the faith, we can look at our past unafraid and from its insights eagerly face the future with new possibilities.[7]

How then do senior clergy and personnel committees introduce an annual process that builds hope and develops alignment in the life of the congregation? Let's look at the possibilities.

The Appraisal Process

There are three distinct types of reviews, each involving a different approach to evaluating performance: top-down reviews, peer reviews, and 360-degree reviews. Regardless of which type of system is chosen, it is important to incorporate some element of self-assessment.[8]

In a top-down review, the person who provides direct oversight of the employee is responsible for the employee's appraisal and has the authority to set a developmental plan for the future. The person who prepares and delivers the appraisal may consult with others in the congregation to get feedback on the evaluation. This is the most conventional type of review used in congregational settings because it is the most straightforward and simplest to administer.

In a peer-review process, people at the same level review their peers so that each reviewer can use his or her expert knowledge of the employee's roles and responsibilities to give an authoritative opinion on the employee's skills. Peer review most often is used in professional positions where a specialized knowledge base makes it useful. Examples of organizations that use a peer-review process include legal firms, consulting organizations, and teaching staffs. By monitoring colleagues as part of the review process, changes in practice can be fed back to the organization and improvements made in the way members behave and work. Peer review is not often used in congregational life for several reasons. First, it is difficult to find a peer group with shared subject matter expertise that can evaluate your staff members. Second, if a staff member has someone who provides direct oversight on a daily basis, that member is not likely to feel satisfied with a peer evaluation. People need to have formal feedback from the person who provides them with day-to-day direction. Peer review may augment top-down feedback but cannot replace it.

The third form of appraisal, which is growing in popularity, is the 360-degree review. In this type of review, the reviewer seeks feedback from every level of the congregation that has interacted with the staff member. This might include a sample of other staff members, board members, trustees, members of the congregation, and people outside of the congregational system. Generally, the employee or reviewer will send out forms or questionnaires and then take comments into account when preparing for the formal review. A 360-degree appraisal can provide rich perspectives that enhance the feedback process. These perspectives are particularly helpful in situations where the relationship between supervisor and subordinate are strained. The reviewee may be suspicious of feedback that comes from a strained relationship. He or she may be more inclined to accept feedback that comes from a broader base of input.

Bear in mind that 360-degree reviews are cumbersome to administer. If the senior clergy or personnel committee is already feeling overwhelmed by the appraisal process, this may not be the best option to consider. A format for a simple 360-degree feedback form is included at the end of this chapter. It is best to start simply and enhance the system as you become more sophisticated in your evaluation techniques.

Whichever appraisal approach is selected, it is important to involve the staff member in some level of self-assessment during the preparatory phase of the review process. Self-assessment encourages employees to play an active role in the review. People tend to be harder on themselves than their supervisor is. This allows the supervisor to offer a positive perspective on the staff member's performance, pointing out areas of strength that the staff member did not recognize.

The easiest and perhaps most effective way to solicit a self-assessment is to give a blank copy of the performance appraisal tool to the staff member and have him or her complete it prior to meeting with the supervisor. The staff member can either submit it to the supervisor ahead of time so that his or her perspective is considered as the supervisor completes his or her form or can bring it to the appraisal meeting to compare with the supervisor's completed form during the review session itself. The former alternative allows the supervisor to anticipate and plan for potential areas of conflict. The latter tends to provoke more honest dialogue between the reviewer and reviewee.

As the appraisal process is selected, attention also needs to be given to what role a parish-staff committee or personnel committee might play in the evaluation process. If a church has a department that operates in a human resource function or a lay committee that provides that function, their help in the planning and administration of the process should be incorporated. Such a committee might be responsible for initiating the process each year, designing the review forms, and coaching staff members who need to deliver the appraisals. The committee or department should not actually complete the review or conduct the review meeting. The person who provides regular oversight to a staff member's daily work always should be the person who delivers the review. To do otherwise confuses lines of authority and accountability in the congregation.

The Appraisal Form

The format of the appraisal form itself can make all the difference between creating a review meeting that is positive and change-focused and one that is negative and judgmental in tone. It is common for a congregation to already have access to performance appraisal forms—either from the archives of the congregation or from a denominational body. A sample copy of a performance appraisal format is included at the end of this chapter. It is important that the congregation evaluate and adapt the form before beginning to review staff members. Be certain that the format adopted does not automatically place the supervisor or your staff member in a negative state of mind before arriving at the appraisal meeting.

There are several dos and don'ts to consider in the selection or design of a performance evaluation tool. Do make certain that:

- the evaluation tool addresses the "real" responsibilities, traits, and attributes of the job that is being performed, not generic ministry categories
- the evaluation tool is consistent with the required responsibilities, traits, and attributes of the job as described in the staff member's job description

- there is plenty of room on the form to include concrete behavioral examples of performance that are to be encouraged or discouraged
- there is a place on the form for establishing future performance and ministry goals

In selecting your performance evaluation tool, try to avoid or steer clear of the following potential pitfalls:

Pitfalls

- Avoid forms that are supposed to evaluate any kind of ministry in any kind of context. Generic forms inevitably lead you down the path of evaluating staff on things over which they have no control or things that are irrelevant to the performance of their ministry.
- Never force rank your employees—that is, never rank them first, second, third, and so on according to performance effectiveness. Force ranking of employees serves no real purpose—even for determining pay increases. Do not select an evaluation tool that goes down that path.
- Be wary of rating systems, especially ones that use arbitrary descriptors of performance acceptability. A common rating scheme that often is lethal in the evaluation meeting is: poor, unacceptable, average, above average, and excellent. What is an average employee? How will any of these designations be objectively justified to the employee? What is average to one leader may well have been considered above average by his or her predecessor. The use of such ratings often leads to a simmering resentment on the part of a staff member. He may have been comfortable and accepting of the narrative examples provided about his performance. And he may even have acknowledged the need to strengthen a skill set or to grow in a specific area of performance—until an average rating was imposed on him. Now all the staff person will think about for the next two months is how his supervisor had the audacity to call him an average performer.

If a rating system is believed to be important to communicate performance levels, select a system that invites further dialogue

and avoids labeling the person. For example, the following ranking system invites dialogue between the supervisor and the staff
member: consistently performs below performance expectation,
often performs below performance expectations, generally meets
performance expectations, often exceeds performance expectations,
and consistently exceeds performance expectations. These ratings do
not automatically suggest fault on the part of the employee. They
invite dialogue around the reasonableness of expectations and how
the employee feels about those expectations.

Delivering the Appraisal: Leading from Strength

Delivering the appraisal from a position of strength does not suggest
that inadequacies are minimized or glossed over. One of the objectives of the annual appraisal is for the supervisor and the employee
to build an honest mutual assessment of his or her leadership potential. Weaknesses need to be talked about to create action plans
for augmenting those weaknesses if the staff member is to thrive.
Do not avoid discussing weakness; instead, reframe the weakness
in light of a corresponding strength. This can be accomplished with
two simple techniques.

First, approach each weakness as an overreliance on—or an
overfunctioning of—a complimentary strength. Many of our weaknesses as managers and leaders emerge because we depend too
heavily on a skill base with which we feel comfortable. We begin
to overfunction in something at which we are accomplished to
compensate for or avoid a weakness in another area. A supervisor
can help a staff member address weakness by approaching his or
her weakness through a corresponding area of strength.

Laurie was an accomplished church office administrator. She
especially was gifted in her ability to manage and measure work
flow. Laurie was good at clearly assigning responsibility for tasks
and decisions. She almost always set precise objectives and measures,
monitored progress and results well, and designed feedback loops
into her work so that she was on pace with projects. Laurie, however,

also was overcontrolling with her volunteer staff. She was always looking over people's shoulders as they did their work, prescribing too much of the workflow, and failing to empower others. If Laurie's head of staff wanted to approach Laurie's weakness from a place of strength, she would help Laurie understand that her "control" problems stemmed from an overreliance on her skills at managing and measuring work flow. Laurie needs help in understanding when to turn off her strong suit and bring in an additional skill set. Talking with Laurie about her difficulty in "letting go" as a natural outgrowth of her managerial strength will help prevent a defensive conversation. It also will give Laurie the confidence she needs to try a new skill set.

Consider another example. Pete is a talented senior adult ministry pastor. One of the things that makes Pete so good at what he does is his extraordinary compassion for the people to whom he ministers. Pete genuinely cares about people. He is concerned about their problems and is always available and ready to help. Pete is especially sympathetic to the plight of others who are not as fortunate as he is and demonstrates real empathy with their joys and pains. When faced with conflict, however, Pete often folds. He tends to smooth over conflict in the interest of harmony. He often is not tough enough in situations that require accountability, yielding too many concessions. Pete sometimes gets so close to people that his objectivity is affected, and they are able to get away with too much. Pete's head of staff can help Pete grapple with this weakness by showing him that his difficulty with conflict is really a manifesta- tion of his gift of compassion. Pete is so good at delivering compassion that he does not always know when to turn it off and when to require accountability. If the critique of his conflict management skills comes out of a dialogue about his skills in compassion, Pete is more likely to accept the critique with grace and courage and be willing to try something different.

A second technique that can be used to approach appraisal from a place of strength is to make clear distinctions between elements of substandard performance that are attributable to the employee and those that are attributable to the environment. Too often employees feel blamed for situations and problems that reside outside of their sphere of influence or control. Even if staff members bear some level of responsibility for failed performance, they are not likely to own their portion of the problem unless their staff leader clearly acknowledges that a part of the problem rests someplace else.

In 1978 Thomas Gilbert developed a Behavior Engineering Model (BEM) that provides organizations with a systematic way to identify barriers to individual performance.[9] The BEM distinguishes between what an individual brings to the performance equation and what the environment brings to bear. A congregational adaptation of that model is presented below.

	Information/ Knowledge	Resources/ Capacity	Motivation
Environment	Roles and performance expectations are clearly defined. Staff receives frequent feedback about the adequacy of performance. Clear expectations have been set regarding expected and acceptable work process.	Materials, tools, and time needed to engage the ministry are present. Processes and procedures have been clearly defined and enhance individual performance if followed. Overall physical and psychological work environment contributes to effective performance.	Financial incentives are fairly administered. Nonfinancial incentives exist and reinforce positive performance. Overall work environment is positive. Staff believes they have the opportunity to succeed and develop their skills.

	Information/ Knowledge	Resources/ Capacity	Motivation
Individual	Staff member has the necessary knowledge, experience, skills, and abilities to do the expected job. Staff member is properly placed to use and share the knowledge, skills, and abilities he/she has.	Staff member has the capacity to learn and do what is needed to perform successfully. Staff member's gifts have been appropriately matched to the work situation in which he or she has been placed. Staff member is free of emotional limitations that might interfere with performance.	Staff member desires to perform the required tasks. Staff member believes that his or her work grows out of a "sense of call" that is honored in this context. Staff member's goals are aligned with the goals of the work, the organization, and the head of staff.

These designations are helpful to the staff leader during the preparation and delivery of the performance appraisal. When preparing the evaluation, take care to identify weaknesses and failures that occurred in the environment that was supposed to support the individual. During the evaluation, ask the staff member to talk about what accountability she can claim personally in the problem. If the staff member still does not want to acknowledge any form of personal responsibility, you can take her through all three categories of personal accountability to discover where she feels she could use some supervisory assistance.

In short, the delivery of the performance evaluation can be hopeful, positive, and change focused. Take care to build on an employee's strengths, and take care not to hold him or her accountable for problems over which he or she has no control.

Linking Performance and Pay

Inevitably the question arises, "Should we tie performance evaluation and salary administration together? If so, how?" The answer is a complex one in any organizational setting, but it is particularly difficult in congregational settings. More often than not, congregations are facing a scarcity of resources that do not allow them to build in much more than a cost-of-living increase. Additionally, those drawn to work in a congregation usually are not drawn by income potential. Money is not likely to function as a motivator for changed performance in congregational settings.

There are several important motivational theories that have something to say about the connection between compensation and performance. In general the consensus of behavioral scientists is moving away from a system that tries to link pay and performance. A growing consensus is emerging that performance needs to be linked to other types of motivators to provide for effective management.

The first motivational theory that bears relevance is Frederick Herzberg's Two Factor Theory of Motivation.[10] In studying the nature of work motivation, Herzberg and his colleagues interviewed more than four thousand employees and asked them to talk about times on the job when they felt exceptionally good or bad about the job. The research team began to see a clear pattern emerge. When people expressed satisfaction with their job, they described a predictable list of things they liked. Herzberg calls these items "satisfiers" or "motivators." They include things like achievement, recognition, the work itself, responsibility, advancement, and growth. These are the components of a work situation that can motivate an employee. Interestingly enough, when it came to expressing dissatisfaction with their jobs, people did not list the absence of satisfiers; they described an entirely different set of factors that Herzberg terms "dissatisfiers" or "maintenance factors." This list includes salary, policy and administration, supervision, relationship with their supervisor, working conditions, relationships with peers, and relationships with subordinates. Herzberg points out that if you correct a problem with one of the maintenance factors, the best that you will get is an employee who is "not dissatisfied" about his or her workplace setting. You cannot get a motivated staff member by adjusting one of the dissatisfiers; motivation only results from working with the satisfiers.

Put another way, a lousy work environment and poor pay can lower motivation, but a superb work environment and great pay cannot create it. It is impossible to design a pay system that will motivate your staff. You, however, can create a pay structure that demotivates or demoralizes your staff.

An additional behavioral theory that merits our attention is Adams's Equity Theory. J. Stacy Adams's theory is staked on the premise that we compare what we do and receive with what others do and receive. If we feel an inequity as a result of that comparison, the response can become a powerful factor in determining our own motivational levels. Adams's equation for equity is straightforward (see figure 9.1 below).[11]

Figure 9.1

$$\frac{\text{My Reward}}{\text{My Input}} \quad \text{Should Equal} \quad \frac{\text{Your Reward}}{\text{Your Input}}$$

When the two sides of the equation balance, we are satisfied and proceed to respond to our usual set of motivators. But when the balance tilts heavily against us, we often act out our frustration and sense of injustice.

Staff member responses can take several forms to restore the balance of the equation. First, they may decide to reduce their input (i.e., effort, involvement, leadership) to produce what they consider to be a more equitable effort/reward ratio. They may try to increase something on the reward side. They may decide to wipe the board clean entirely by quitting. They also may try to impact the equation by getting the other person to work harder or receive less of a reward.

What does all of this have to do with linking a congregation's evaluation system and its compensation system? It suggests that the decisions you make in your congregation relative to salary must be managed carefully to produce a sense of fairness in how people are rewarded. It is very difficult to produce a system that rewards degrees of good performance. Such a system, even if it were administered fairly, would produce negligible motivational impact. Leaders, however, do need to make certain that salary rewards reflect some level of distinction between acceptable and unacceptable performers. A system that is perceived as unfair can wreak havoc with all of your attempts at positive performance assessment.

Sample Performance Evaluation

Employee's Name: Mary Mostly
Social Security Number: 555-55-5555
Position Title: Director of Small Group Ministry
Supervisor's Name: John Justin
Supervisor's Title: Pastor of Discipleship
Date of Review: 9/01/05
Period Reviewed: 9/06–8/07

1. Accomplishments (List the employee's major accomplishments during this review period.)

    A.

    B.

    C.

    D.

2. Essential Functions and Responsibilities (The content of this section corresponds to the section of the same name in the employee's job description.)

Rating Scale:
1 = Unacceptable (Does not meet requirements)
2 = Needs Improvement (Meets some but not all requirements)
3 = Meets Expectations (Consistently meets requirements)
4 = Exceeds Expectations (Meets all expectations and exceeds some)
5 = Outstanding (Consistently exceeds all expectations)

Performance Expectations Taken from job description	Comments Describe how performance compares with expectations. Describe strengths and areas for improvement.	Rating (1–5)
Creates and communicates a vision for small group ministries.		
Develops a network of spiritually gifted coaches, leaders, mentors, and apprentices who can disciple people toward spiritual maturity in small group settings.		
Develops and maintains a resource library of small group curriculum.		
Coordinates and facilitates small group leader training events.		
Designs and promotes creative small group celebrations.		

Performance Expectations Taken from job description	Comments Describe how performance compares with expectations. Describe strengths and areas for improvement.	Rating (1–5)
Maintains a database and Web site for small groups at ABC.		
Develops a program for evaluating the performance of small group leaders and the functioning of their groups.		

3. Core Competencies (The content of this section corresponds to the section of the same name in the employee's job description. This section of the performance review is narrative only. Performance ratings are not assigned.)

Competency Taken from job description	Comment Provide examples of behavioral strengths. Describe behaviors that need to be added to employee's competency base.
Organizing: Can gather and organize resources (people, funding, material, support) to get things done; can orchestrate multiple activities at once to accomplish a goal; uses resources effectively and efficiently.	
Planning: Accurately assesses the length and difficulty of a project; sets objectives and goals; breaks down work into process steps; develops schedules and task/people assignments; anticipates and adjusts for problems and roadblocks; measures performance against goals; evaluates results.	

Competency Taken from job description	Comment Provide examples of behavioral strengths. Describe behaviors that need to be added to employee's competency base.
Managing Vision and Purpose: Articulates and supports the vision and mission of ABC Church; communicates a compelling and inspired vision for ministry; talks beyond the here and now to a larger sense of purpose; creates a compelling vision of possibility, hope, and optimism; creates mileposts and symbols to rally support behind the vision; helps others to own the vision.	
Developing Volunteers: Is able to identify raw talent and recruit capable people into positions of responsibility; provides challenging and stretching tasks and assignments for others to do; delegates appropriately; builds people up; maintains open and active dialogue with volunteers; communicates expectations clearly and holds people accountable.	
Managing Conflict: Deals with problems quickly and directly; steps up to conflicts, seeing them as opportunities; reads situations quickly; good at focused listening; settles disputes collaboratively and equitably; finds common ground and gets cooperation.	
Interpersonal Relationships: Relates well to all kinds of people, inside and outside of the congregation; builds appropriate rapport; builds effective and constructive relationships; uses diplomacy and tact; regarded as a team player.	

Competency Taken from job description	Comment Provide examples of behavioral strengths. Describe behaviors that need to be added to employee's competency base.
Trust and Integrity: Is widely trusted; seen as direct and truthful; keeps confidences; admits mistakes; adheres to an appropriate and effective set of core values during good and bad times; acts in line with those values; practices what he/she preaches.	

4. Goals for the Coming Year (These should be aligned with the congregation's goals.)

   A.

   B.

   C.

   D.

   Employee's Comments

Employee's Signature _____
Date _____
Supervisor's Signature _____
Date _____

Sample Feedback Form
360-Degree Appraisal Format

The employee to be appraised actually addresses the forms to reviewers whom he or she has selected for input. Reviewers are instructed to return the form to the employee's supervisor, who then will summarize and share the results with the employee being evaluated. This format can be used anonymously or with names attached.

Employee Being Evaluated: _____

Employee Sharing Observations: _____

Please answer the following questions as briefly and concisely as possible:

1. What part of my performance as _____ do you think I should continue doing?

2. What part of my performance should I stop doing?

3. What am I currently not doing that I should start doing?

Source: Adele Margrave and Robert Gordon, Performance Appraisals (New York: Penguin, 2001), 278.

PART 3
Special Topics in the
Supervisory Relationship

Chapter 10

Staff Team Design

Moses heard the people of every family wailing, each at the entrance to his tent. The LORD became exceedingly angry, and Moses was troubled. He asked the LORD, "Why have you brought this trouble on your servant? What have I done to displease you that you put the burden of all these people on me? Did I conceive all these people? Did I give them birth? Why do you tell me to carry them in my arms, as a nurse carries an infant, to the land you promised on oath to their forefathers? Where can I get meat for all these people? They keep wailing to me, 'Give us meat to eat!' I cannot carry all these people by myself; the burden is too heavy for me. If this is how you are going to treat me, put me to death right now—if I have found favor in your eyes—and do not let me face my own ruin."

The LORD said to Moses: "Bring me seventy of Israel's elders who are known to you as leaders and officials among the people. Have them come to the Tent of Meeting, that they may stand there with you. I will come down and speak with you there, and I will take of the Spirit that is on you and put the Spirit on them. They will help you carry the burden of the people so that you will not have to carry it alone."

Numbers 11:10-17

What congregational leader can't relate to the figure of Moses in this passage—the weariness of caring for a faith community, anger with the Lord for being left in charge of such a disorganized mess, relief at being told that others will share the leadership burden. How long do you suppose Moses's sense of relief lasted upon the appointment of the seventy elders? If Moses's leadership experience parallels our own, his relief was likely short-lived. Only moments would have passed before Moses felt the new burden of having seventy eager managers who needed to be organized and equipped for the ministry laid before them.

Every pastor of a large congregation has shared this Moses moment—gratitude for the staff team that God has assembled to do the ministry of the congregation coupled with panic and confusion about how that team ought to be organized. Pastor Gretchen knows that experience only too well. Gretchen has been head of staff at Faith Church for seven years. Her first year as head of staff was a time of watching and learning. She didn't make many changes to the staffing configuration. But then things started to evolve. Two key staff leaders left, partly in response to Gretchen's leadership style, which was significantly more collaborative than her predecessor's. The time seemed ripe for reorganization, and Gretchen used these departures to mix things up a bit. Job descriptions were rewritten, staff members were assigned new reporting relationships, and Gretchen was hopeful that the new configuration would help bring about a long overdue cultural shift in the congregation. Instead, confusion emerged. The new reporting relationships didn't make sense to some of the longer tenured staff members, who basically decided to ignore them and go about their work as they always had. Several significant communication and decision-making glitches occurred during a six-month period, and Gretchen decided that further tweaking of the structure was needed. Over the following three-year period, the structure was tweaked a total of five times. But things still aren't working smoothly, and the continual reorganization has become something of a joke among staff members. Gretchen is willing to admit defeat. Exactly what is it that she is supposed to be paying attention to with regard to her staffing structure? What are the basic principles that need to be honored in the crafting of a staff team design?

Moses was working from the ground up to build an organizational structure where none existed. Gretchen had to work with a broken structure inherited from a predecessor. Both leaders had to grapple with the same core design decisions. At the core of every decision about staffing configuration are four basic design features that need to be addressed and resolved:

1. basis for division of labor
2. mechanisms for integrating the work
3. level of centralization in decision making
4. span of control established for leaders

Let's walk through each of these issues in more detail to illustrate what both Moses and Gretchen were evaluating as they made decisions about organizational design.

Basis for Division of Labor

The first decision that Moses faced in trying to organize the work of the seventy elders had to be a question about the division of labor. How would the work that needed to be accomplished be divided among the available workers? And how would those divided tasks be grouped together? These two questions form the essence of division of labor. Moses could have simply seated the seventy in a circle and told them to wait for the emerging need to shape their work, but that would have produced a highly inefficient and chaotic organizational system. In Exodus 18 we learn that Moses designated these leaders as "officials over thousands, hundreds, fifties and tens" (v. 21). In other words, he assigned the people into meaningful groups of some kind and then appointed leaders over each group. Every time Moses assigned a leader to a group of people, he was making a decision about division of labor. He was making determinations about the nature of specialization his leaders would develop and about the focus of their work. Let's examine the variety of options he would have had available to him as he made those choices.

First, Moses could have made a decision to organize his workers horizontally, according to function or process. In this type of structure, jobs are grouped at the same level of the hierarchy, according to processes or functional needs of the community. In Moses's situation we might imagine that a functional organizational chart, with a horizontal orientation would have looked something like this:

Horizontal (Functional) Approach

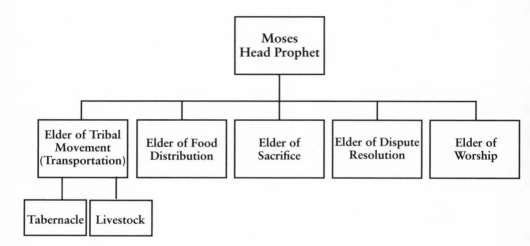

In a structure with a *horizontal* orientation, functions are added on the same organizational level as the needs of the community grow. The organizational design remains largely flat. So if the community suddenly sensed a need for leadership in the area of property allocation, an elder would be added to the same level of the chart as the other elders. Additional levels of the organization might emerge below this one, but they would emerge according to the functional demands defined by the first reporting level immediately under the leader. Perhaps the elder of transportation would have someone reporting to him who oversaw the transportation of the tabernacle. Another of his staff members might oversee the transportation of livestock, and so on.

The advantage of a horizontal structure is that people stay well connected to the vision of the leader. Not much goes on without the knowledge or involvement of the primary leader. Of course, this is also the weakness of a horizontal structure. The size of the organization will be limited by the oversight capacity of its primary leader. As the organization grows in size, the leadership team experiences more instances of failed communication as the leader struggles to keep pace with the number of direct relationships that must be managed. This type of structure also struggles with communication barriers between functional areas. Each functional area tends to develop a silo mentality, seeing itself as distinct from each of the other functional areas.

A second option for division of labor is to take a *vertical* approach to design. An organization with a vertical orientation might also be thought of as a tall organization. This type of design builds checks and balances into the system by adding levels of oversight. Tall structures provide natural lines of advancement for employees and extra capacity for introducing quality into the system. Furthermore, natural linkages in decision making and communication occur between functional areas that have shared reporting oversight. However, a disadvantage of vertical organizations is that they tend to be slower at decision making and they do not develop critical decision-making skills at lower levels of the organization. They are less flexible and adaptable than horizontal organizations; the taller the structure, the longer it takes to work change through the system. Had Moses used a vertical differentiation approach for organizing his elders, the structure might have looked something like this.

Vertical Approach

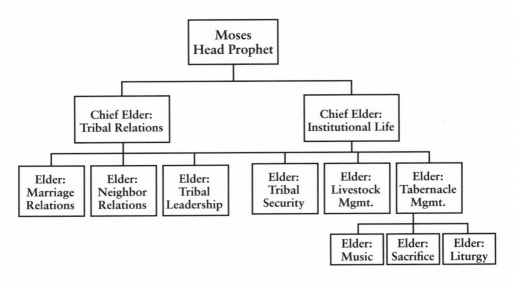

Finally, as Moses grappled with the division of labor question among his new elders, he might have taken a *spatial* approach. This approach groups leaders and workers according to geographical locations (or according to the natural groupings of constituents) being served. The strength of this type of structure is that it allows leaders to respond very effectively to the unique needs of their constituency groups. Organizations with spatial structures tend to be very flexible and adaptable. A disadvantage is that they may have built-in redundancies. In an effort to serve the needs of their unique constituencies, leaders often reinvent functions and processes already offered in other areas of the organization. We don't know what type of organizational design Moses employed. However, the heavy emphasis on tribal life in Scripture may suggest that elder leadership was organized using a spatial design.

Spatial Approach

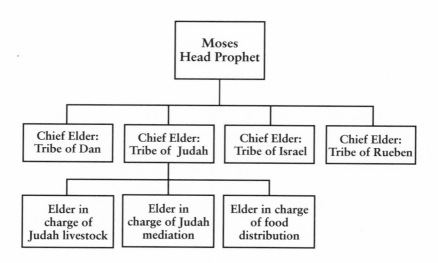

Ultimately the choice that a leader makes about the division of labor on the staff team should be reflective of the mission of the congregation. In Moses's case, he led a faith community that was intrinsically formed by tribal identity. Creating a design structure for leadership that honored those tribal differences would have been imperative. As you make decisions about the division of labor on your staff team, you also need to consider what is unique about your context, the constituencies you serve, and the values you embrace. Every organizational design has both strengths and weaknesses. You want to select a division of labor that suits the unique strengths and capabilities of your context.

Integrating Mechanisms

Once an organization has created positions and some logical grouping of those positions, it must find ways to coordinate the work of the groupings it has produced. Integration refers to the extent and means by which an organization holds together its various parts and helps them work together to accomplish a shared goal. In chapter 3 we addressed the need for the staff to have a defined and shared sense of outcomes. Chapter 9 on performance evaluation explains how alignment is accomplished through the performance review process, and chapter 11 on staff meetings explains how alignment is strengthened within the dynamics of a well-run staff meeting. In this chapter we will focus on the design elements that contribute to a shared sense of purpose. The primary ways that an organization's design can contribute to the coordination of work efforts is through mutual adjustment, shared direct supervision, and the standardization of processes.[1]

Mutual adjustments are the informal but direct communication links that develop between individuals within the organization. For example, the youth director and children's director meet over coffee once a week to talk about family dynamics that are impacting students in their ministries. The amount of mutual adjustment within a staffing structure is as much a function of the culture of an organization as its design. However, a poor organizational design can prevent natural communication links from developing by creating arbitrary barriers. If people have to spend inordinate amounts of time jumping through hoops to honor meaningless structural relationships, they will be less likely to develop authentic informal relationships with one another.

Shared direct supervision creates linkages within your system. When a supervisor has direct responsibility for two or more employees, the grouping of employees that he or she supervises will form natural linkages to one another. If the youth director and children's director both report to the same supervisor, they are more likely to coordinate their work, either in joint meetings with that supervisor or informally, because both are operating from the same set of shared expectations. Each of these direct reports receives consistent messages about vision, approach, and outcomes because each goes back to the same source. When you want to build a natural linkage between two parts of your system, try to have those parts share the same direct reporting relationship.

Standardization of work processes. Two functions within your congregation that share the same database are more likely to develop natural connections with one another than two functions that develop their own systems. Likewise, two functions that share a common leadership development pool will form natural points of connection. If the youth director and the children's director both engage the same processes for tracking attendance and participation, their work will more naturally align, because both will be operating with a shared set of data. Creating shared work processes will encourage the development of organizational connections between different parts of your system.

Centralization of Decision Making

The third major dimension of organizational design that should influence your staff team design is the extent to which you desire centralized or decentralized decision making. In a centralized structure, decision making is limited to the top post(s). In a decentralized structure, the responsibility for decision making is disseminated throughout the organization.

Jethro instructed Moses that he should "be the people's representative before God and bring their disputes to him . . . but select capable men . . . and appoint them as officials" (Exod. 18:19-21).

They should serve as judges over the ordinary but should "bring every difficult case to [Moses]." In offering this advice, Jethro was finding language to talk about the centralization of decision making in the emerging nation. Certain decisions would still be centralized and reside with Moses; others would be decentralized and shared among the elders.

Certain organizational designs will reinforce a centralized approach to decision making. The more vertical the organization, the greater the degree of centralized decision making. The flatter an organization, the greater the degree of decentralization. Why is this? The layers of an organization are decision-making repositories. The middle levels of organizations exist primarily to handle out-of-the-ordinary decision making and problem solving. When we reduce the number of levels in the structure, employees at all levels are forced to take on more decision-making responsibility.

Span of Control

The fourth and final dimension of organizational design is the managerial span of control. What is the optimum number of people and functions that a supervisor can oversee effectively? This question is basically concerned with the volume of interpersonal relationships that a supervisor can reasonably expect to maintain. As Moses made decisions about the groupings of tens, fifties, hundreds, and thousands, he was also grappling with determinations about span of control.

Pastors frequently pose this question during a consultation: What is the ideal number of people that any one supervisor should oversee? The answer is always the same: it depends. The answer is different for every organization and for different parts of the same organization, so there is no easily prescribed answer. However, the factors that should be considered in making that determination form a great discussion outline.

As you consider the span of control for any individual manager, you need to consider both the number of formal and informal relationships that the supervisor is likely to have. This is important because the number of potential interpersonal relationships between a manager and subordinates increases geometrically as the number of subordinates increases arithmetically. Managers have to handle three types of relationships among their direct reports. First, they manage the one-on-one relationship between themselves and the direct subordinate. Second, they manage their relationship with the group as a whole. Third, they manage the interpersonal relationships that unfold among members of their team. Collectively this leads to a complex web of relationships that must be considered within the span-of-control question.[2]

Considering the span of control requires thinking about the level of contact a particular group of subordinates needs. Employees who need more oversight will need to work for managers who have fewer direct reports. Greater one-on-one contact time is required for roles that have a greater level of ambiguity in design. Greater one-on-one contact time is also generally required for staff members who are newer on the job. Supervisors who oversee these types of employees need to have fewer direct reports.

Jobs at lower levels of the organization tend to be more specialized and less complicated than jobs higher in the organization. Supervisors at lower levels of the organization can generally oversee the work of more employees because the jobs they are overseeing are less complex. At higher levels of the organization, roles tend to become much broader and less specialized. Overseeing jobs at this level requires a much greater scope of knowledge and information. The higher you go in the organization, the fewer the number of direct reports that can be supervised effectively.

Finally, the ease of communication between the leader and subordinates will determine the number of direct reports. If some of the employees the leader oversees are located at another physical site, work on a different schedule, or come from a different cultural background, it may be difficult to establish easy lines of communication. Reduce the number of direct reports an employee is responsible for if the lines of communication between supervisor and subordinate are difficult for any reason.

These four major dimensions of organizational design—division of labor, integrating mechanisms, centralization of decision making, and span of control—have helped us analyze the situation Moses faced with the sudden appointment of seventy new elders. It is helpful to use these four dimensions when thinking about the design of a totally new organization. But let us turn back to Pastor Gretchen and her situation at Faith Church. Gretchen wasn't faced with designing a brand-new system. She inherited a system that wasn't working for her leadership style. How should Gretchen approach the evaluation of her staff team design? Do the same dimensions and questions apply?

The dimensions of organizational design have relevance whether the structure to be created is brand-new or in need of reconfiguration. However, Susan has sometimes found it more effective to deal with a specialized set of questions when evaluating existing church staffing structures. The following ten questions address the four elements of organizational design discussed above, but they do so through very specific exploratory approaches. These particular questions can help to focus attention on the adequacy of a structure's capacity for growth, the organizational fit of the design, and the effectiveness of the design.[3]

The staffing configuration that Gretchen is currently using at Faith Church is presented in figure 10.4 on the next page. The following pages will illustrate the application of the ten evaluative questions with Faith Church's staff team configuration as a case study. Please turn to the organizational design before reading any further. Think about the design through the lens of the four dimensions of design that we have already explored. When you are ready, resume your reading to see how the ten evaluative questions might be used to reflect on Gretchen's staff configuration.

Figure 10.4
Faith Church Staff Team

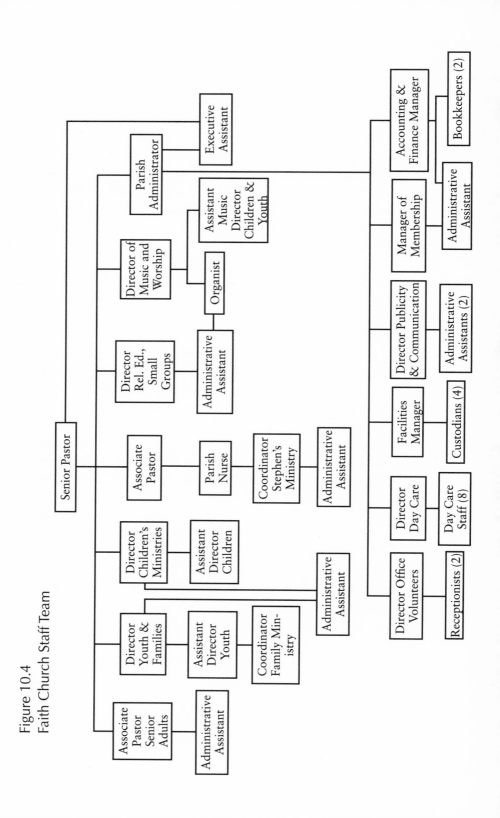

Capacity Questions

1. Are we adequately staffed for our size and growth aspirations?
Two resources are generally cited when grappling with issues of congregational staffing capacity. *The Multiple Staff and the Larger Church* by Lyle Schaller[4] and *Staff Your Church for Growth: Building Team Ministry in the 21st Century* by Gary McIntosh[5] each provide extensive guidelines for determining the correct size staff for your congregation. We won't attempt to repeat their work here in any significant way. Suffice it to say that both authors look at staff size through the lens of average weekend worship attendance. The size of the program staff will generally determine the congregation's ability to connect with active members and provide outreach to potential new members. Schaller advocates the equivalent of one full-time professional program staff position for every one hundred people in average worship attendance. McIntosh makes an argument for a ratio of 1:150. Both authors are quick to qualify those numbers on the basis of program complexity and level of staff specialization.

Faith Church, under Gretchen's strong leadership, has grown to a weekend worshiping community of 950. Worship attendance has grown by 18 percent in the seven years since Gretchen's arrival, and the church council has set a targeted growth goal of 25 percent over the next five years. Is the current staffing configuration adequate to support this growth goal? Six of the direct reports to Gretchen would qualify as full-time program staff (the director of music and worship counts, the parish administrator and executive assistant do not). Additionally, five part-time employees at the assistant level would translate into two full-time program staff equivalents. Counting Gretchen as a full-time program staff member, Faith Church has a total of nine full-time equivalent program staff employees. Schaller would say that this size program staff team is sufficient to meet the needs of a nine-hundred-person weekend worshiping community. McIntosh argues that this staff team should be able to support growth up to 1,350. Gretchen's program staff team appears to have an appropriate number of professionals devoted to building the programs of the church.

The other capacity feature of staffing to consider is the level of administrative office support available for program staff. McIntosh asserts that, in general, one administrative assistant is needed for every two full-time program staff members to work to their capacity. Again, this general guideline must be adapted in light of program specialization and complexity. This general guideline suggests that Faith Church should be functioning with 4.5 full-time administrative assistants supporting program staff. Gretchen's program staff currently utilizes five full-time administrative assistants. While the number of assistants appears sufficient, the allocation of those assistants is somewhat questionable. The associate pastor of senior adults has his own assistant. Does this assistant overfunction as another half-time program staff member, or is there a more political reason for this provision? Is the associate pastor underperforming in his role, requiring a fully dedicated administrative assistant? Meanwhile the religious education, outreach and worship functions of the church all share one administrative support person. Is this adequate support for such a variety of ministries?

Above all, it is important to bear in mind that all of these guidelines are simply that—guidelines. Ultimately, Faith Church has to examine what is working and what is not working in the staffing structure in light of its mission and ministry. The Alban Institute regularly encounters thriving congregations whose staffing configurations fall significantly outside of these guidelines. The guidelines are useful for framing dialogue, but ultimately Faith Church must be staffed in a manner that feels right to them.

2. Can we afford a staff team designed for growth?

Figuring out the right size program team to support and sustain congregational growth is an important component of capacity. However, the companion question that must be addressed is whether the congregation can underwrite its ideal sized staff team and still afford to finance other important aspects of its ministry. The primary way to evaluate the affordability of the staff team is by looking at payroll expense as a percentage of operating budget. The Alban Institute generally recommends that total payroll expense fall somewhere between 40 and 60 percent of the total operating budget. The congregation with a payroll budget below this amount may be seriously understaffed for the level of programming it needs. A congregation that exceeds this range may find that specific programs, outreach, or building needs are not satisfied because too much of the budget is allocated to payroll.

Faith Church has an annual operating budget of $3.8 million. Total payroll expense last year (including benefits) was $2,175,000. This represented 57 percent of the total operating budget. Faith is pushing the upper limits of affordability with its staffing configuration. However, this is entirely appropriate for a congregation that is expecting sustained growth and plans to achieve that growth through program-oriented ministries. Leadership at Faith will have to continually monitor other key components of its operating budget to insure that specific programs, the building plant, and mission giving are not shortchanged by payroll commitments.

3. Do we have an appropriate balance between staff members with a relational outreach and those with an institutional caretaking orientation?

As congregations grow in size and complexity, they need to provide a blend of positions that will balance both the relationship and task dimensions of congregational life, as well as the internal and external dimensions of church life. As congregations age, there is a natural tendency to devote increasing amounts of time and energy toward the institutional aspect of congregational life and toward the needs and wants of existing membership. If staff teams are not carefully designed, there may be a natural tendency to provide institutional caretaking at the expense of outreach and growth.

Any staff team design can be evaluated for a balance between these two dimensions of congregational life. How much of each staff member's time is focused primarily on relational outreach? How much time is focused on institutional caretaking? Positions can't always be neatly assigned to one category or the other, as many positions carry a dual focus. You may want to consider having each member of your staff team estimate how much of his or her time is spent on internally focused caretaking and how much is spent on externally focused outreach. Your associate minister in charge of pastoral care may understandably be spending 85 percent of his time focused internally on the needs of the congregation. Your youth director may be spending 60 percent of her time on outreach and growth, while the administrative pastor spends fully 100 percent of her time on institutional concerns. In general, the collective staff team needs to devote balanced attention to both sides of congregational life.

At Faith Church an analysis of staff positions indicates that the equivalent of eleven full-time positions are devoted to relational outreach and the equivalent of fifteen full-time positions are focused more institutionally. Is this balance reasonable? Only the leadership at Faith Church can answer that question after careful consideration of their strengths, weaknesses, congregational mission, and strategic priorities. Will this combination of relational and institutional focus provide the right blend of workers to achieve the congregation's particular growth strategy?

Organizational Fit Questions

4. Does the staff design direct sufficient leadership attention to the ministries or features of congregational life that make us unique?
Every congregation has a broad purpose that it shares with all Christian congregations. On some level every congregation is meant to honor and serve God and help members grow in relationship with God and humankind. However, every congregation also has a unique mission that is born of its specific context and giftedness. The configuration of the staff team needs to be evaluated according to its ability to serve the congregation's unique identity. If a congregation believes that social ministry is a distinctive ministry niche, then that emphasis should be readily apparent from looking at the design of the team. Likewise, if a congregation houses a world-class musical program, the staffing configuration will reflect an emphasis in that area of church life.

Faith Church prides itself on being a congregation that caters to families with children. A wide array of children's programming is offered, significant emphasis is placed on the confirmation process, and parents often report feeling very supported by the church on issues of parenting and Christian character formation. Would the reader know this by looking at the staff design of Faith Church?

5. Does the current design reflect the core values of the congregation? Since Pastor Gretchen's arrival, she has been working very hard to integrate participative decision making into every aspect of congregational life. Gretchen's predecessor displayed a decidedly authoritarian, closed decision-making leadership style. Which value system does the current organizational system reinforce? Will this structure encourage or discourage participative decision making and collaborative leadership?

Let's reflect first on whether this design tends to be more vertical or horizontal in focus. Remember that horizontal organizations tend to spread out decision making and vertical organizations tend to concentrate decision making at higher levels of the organization. Faith Church has a fairly flat structure. (Don't be misled by the fact that all of the parish administrator's direct reports appear at the bottom of the page. This really doesn't represent extra layers of the organization. If the page were big enough, these functions would spread out horizontally across the page at a level just below the parish administrator.)

The flat structure is great for introducing the type of participative decision making that Gretchen seeks. However, we also have to remember that flat structures are notorious for creating a silo mentality. This staffing configuration has very few built-in connecting/interfacing mechanisms. It is probably very easy for each staff area to make decisions independently, fly their decision by the senior pastor, and fail to engage any other segment of congregational life. Gretchen might want to consider what could be done to build in more points of connectivity.

This is only one example of a congregational core value that can be analyzed from the perspective of organizational design. Think about the critical core values that you are trying to inculcate into your organization. To what extent is your staff design reinforcing that value or working against it?

Organizational Design Questions

6. Does the design protect specialized ministries that need distinctive cultures to flourish?

Oftentimes, emergent ministries need space for exploration. They need to be nurtured in an environment that allows for different ways of thinking outside of the prevailing congregational norms. Faith Church has two strategic priorities for the next five-year period. The first is to introduce a contemporary worship experience, first on a monthly basis and then weekly. This priority has logically been assigned to the director of music and worship. The second priority is to launch a small group ministry, with the hope that such a ministry will eventually replace a floundering Sunday school program. Small groups currently fall under the jurisdiction of the director of religious education and outreach.

To flourish, both of these strategic priorities are going to require a new cultural ethos. If the current religious education experience of the congregation is dying out, what is the likelihood that the person running that program will have the creative capacity to give birth to small groups? Perhaps he can, but will the congregation expect and allow something new to emerge from that camp? Similarly, can the current director of music and worship who resonates well with a traditional worship venue adequately nourish an alternative worship style? Perhaps both of these strategic priorities would benefit from a temporary reporting relationship that resides outside of the traditional functional area. While the new ministries are being birthed, it may be best to have the responsible staff team member report directly to the senior pastor or another member of the staff team that appreciates the unique cultural requirements.

7. Does the current design foster collaboration for important units with logical linkage to one another?

In some ways this question was addressed when we looked at the issue of the congregation's core values. Let's revisit the question again, this time looking for specific points where linkages occur and other areas where linkages probably should occur. Remember that integrative mechanisms can occur from mutual agreements to collaborate, shared reporting relationships, and standardized processes. The only one of these three mechanisms that can be observed by studying figure 10.4 is shared reporting relationships. The presence or absence of the other mechanisms can only be assumed.

Three areas on the chart reveal shared reporting relationships at the administrative assistant level. This is probably not the strongest level of the organization at which to build shared relationship, but it does provide some interconnectedness. At a minimum, when the administrative assistant has to balance conflicting demands, he has to negotiate his role between both supervisors. If he is a good assistant, he will look for areas of overlap between the two ministries and highlight areas where a mutual body of work appears to be emerging. Currently, the following areas at Faith Church share administrative assistants:

director of youth and families and director of children's
    ministries
director of religious education/outreach and director of music
    and worship
membership ministry and accounting and finance manager

The first of these paired relationships might actually produce some synergistic benefit. There may be considerable overlap between youth, children, and family programming that an assistant could facilitate. The second of the three sets of relationships probably has minimal useful overlap. The third set of relationships may share some record-keeping overlap but may also raise questions about the appropriate separation of duties from an accounting perspective. Should membership ministry have access to giving records?

When searching for logical reporting linkages within a system, it helps to look higher up the reporting chain rather than at the administrative assistant level. If Faith Church is truly interested in building a synergistic children's, youth, and family ministry, they may want to promote one of the current directors to a slightly higher level of oversight. (That person would still carry his or her programmatic responsibilities but would be charged with a collective oversight of the combined function.) Furthermore, they may want to consider having the director of daycare report to the program side of the church rather than through the administrative side of the church. What is the daycare learning about ministering to children and families that never translates over to the program side of the congregation? Are there missed opportunities for outreach to the families of daycare members because of the current reporting relationship? Finally, Faith Church may want to consider a dual reporting relationship for the assistant music director that focuses on youth and children's ministry. Perhaps she should report jointly to the oversight director of children and youth, as well as to the music director.

Another area to consider shared reporting relationships may be in the areas of senior adult ministry and pastoral care. Certainly not all pastoral care is directed at the senior adult population in the congregation, but there are probably significant points of overlap in ministry between these two roles.

8. Does the current design have built-in redundancy?

Redundancy occurs when different parts of the organization have to recreate or reinvent similar roles/functions to meet their ongoing ministry needs. For example, a redundancy would exist if children's ministry and youth ministry designed separate databases to track attendance in their respective programs or entered basic family information twice into a congregational tracking system. Simple analysis of the organizational chart will not reveal whether redundancies currently exist within the system. Redundancy of functions most often occurs when multiple reporting levels are built into a staffing structure. The present, flat organizational design minimizes the likelihood of redundancy at Faith Church. Each time a supervisory layer is added into the organizational chart, the risk of creating more organizational redundancy is increased.

Gretchen has reason to believe, based on personal observation, that there is some redundancy among the administrative assistant roles on the program side of the church. It seems that multiple databases are being maintained to track program involvement and attendance. She may want to conduct a specific study of that role at Faith Church to test her suspicions.

9. Does the design encourage accountability?
Ideally, you want to make certain that the staffing structure assigns legitimate *authority* to each role (the right to assign resources, make decisions, and control the flow of information). You also want to make certain that areas of *responsibility* (the duty to complete tasks) are clearly outlined. Finally, you want to make certain that those who have been assigned responsibility and given authority are *held accountable* for the appropriate completion/outcome of those tasks.

Accountability is easiest to enforce in a system where there is a clear definition of responsibility for separate functional areas of ministry. Can the director of children's ministry be held accountable for successes and failures of the children's Sunday school hour? Who should be held accountable if there is a component of the program that involves music department leadership and some part of the Sunday morning experience that falls under the jurisdiction of the religious education director—the music department, children's ministry, or religious education? Whenever two or more organizational units are jointly responsible for a shared ministry, organizational accountability is likely to be a problem.

10. Is the span of control for each supervisor/manager appropriate?
As previously stated, the span of control refers to the number of people and resources a manager oversees. Remember, when defining the span of control, you need to consider the number of direct reports that an individual has, as well as the informal interpersonal relationships the manager must handle within a staff team.

In considering Faith Church, we have to ask some serious questions about Gretchen's span of control. Gretchen provides direct oversight for seven broad areas of ministry. Additionally she is charged with overall accountability for the new strategic priorities of the congregation, and she is the primary weekend speaker. Gretchen can never abdicate her indirect responsibility for the ministry of the full church, but she can free herself to work more strategically within the church by eliminating some of her direct reporting relationships. As previously suggested, she may choose to elevate several of her more gifted associate pastors or directors to an oversight function. She will want to avoid creating another full level of the organization that is purely administrative by having each of those elevated roles maintain some responsibility for program execution. However, introducing some subtle layering into the staff structure will create development opportunities for staff members and give Gretchen some much needed space to lead the larger institution.

What Is the "Right" Answer?

By now the reader is longing to see a graphic portrayal of the staff team chart for Faith Church that corrects all of the potential problems we have noted in Gretchen's design. At the risk of disappointing the reader, no such chart is being provided. When it comes to the tricky work of staff team design, there are few right answers or formulas to follow. The ten evaluation questions presented here are intended to provoke dialogue among the leaders of a congregation about what might work best in their setting. Ultimately, the leadership of a congregation is the only group that can decide whether the staff team configuration is appropriate. Is it working well? Why? Does it seem broken? What might be changed to make it more effective? In all likelihood, the conversations about staff team design will be more beneficial than whatever chart is drawn to depict that design.

Far too many pastoral leaders are invested in the continual tweaking of their staffing structure, trying to fix problems that may have more to do with individual performance management or congregational culture. Every time the staff team design is changed, potentially radical change is introduced into the system. New reporting relationships require whole new patterns of communication and decision making. If such changes are made easily and thoughtlessly, as in Gretchen's experience, the staff team will begin to ignore the plethora of changes coming their way.

Save major organizational redesign for those moments in the life of the congregation when it is necessary to get the staff team's attention to introduce a radical new day. In the meantime, use the ten questions to host meaningful dialogue about how people ought to be working with one another. If change must be introduced, think about experimenting with small modifications in the way people are asked to work together. Introduce modest refinements in reporting relationships, refine some of the lateral working relationships, refine accountabilities, and introduce new expectations about leadership styles. Save the major reorganizational attempts for times when it is truly necessary to get the attention of your people.

Chapter 11

Staff Meetings

The following is a portion of an e-mail one of us received from an interim senior clergy person who was responsible for addressing issues of staff, structure, and alignment while the congregation prepared to call its new settled leader:

> So, the downward trend in membership has a lot of factors, one of which, I think, is related to the staff's attitude toward being lone rangers. By that I mean they—as I was told in initial interviewing of them—were used to working alone and didn't want to change that. I'm a team kind of guy. . . . I like team members' taking initiative, etc. . . . But one of the things that was not happening at all was staff meetings. I tried to start having them each week and started softly. We started with Bible study and my reflection on it, went to calendar review, then around the circle for comments, updates, creative thinking, as well as making sure all bases were covered for upcoming events.
>
> The personnel committee moderator finally came to me with a list of complaints from staff . . . about the meetings. They were too long, irrelevant, and made them feel like they were being treated like children, and the time with the Bible was remedial. . . .
>
> The ramification is that attempting to broaden outreach and evangelism efforts is not possible as a team coordinated effort. The membership still sees the church as operating under the decision making of the staff, and within their respective areas the staff people keep on making decisions, but there is little or no—mostly

no—coordination. This I believe has been a major contributor to
the decline in participation (membership, giving, etc.).

This pastor was trying to deal with his inherited staff, who had
well-established norms of operating without a cohesive center. The
standard joke about consultants is that they are fiercely independent
and that getting any agreement from them or coordinated decision
making is "like herding cats." The truth is that cats and consultants—and congregational staff members—are only some of the
human and animal types who, if given a choice, will wander and
meander, following their own sense of direction and purpose. Such
wandering or meandering is not functional in a larger congregation
with multiple staff.

One of the primary tools for turning cats toward coordinated
activity and common purpose is the staff meeting. Usually held
on a weekly basis in most large congregations, the staff meeting
is one of the most important disciplines a staff team can practice.
In chapter 3 we spoke of the critical importance of clear outcomes
for a congregation. We invoked the old adage "If you don't know
where you are going, any path will get you there." And we clearly
noted the need for both the congregation and the staff to identify
where they are going and for what they are to be held accountable.
The staff meeting is a primary place to provide a center that offers
both a clearinghouse for information and a point of alignment for
the efforts of all staff members. It is the place to have conversations
about vision, mission, purpose, and how the pieces fit together.

Despite the need for a clear center, many organizations, including
large congregations, are experienced more as a gathering of multiple
initiatives housed—comfortably or uncomfortably—under the same
tent but not always clearly connected. Congregations are human
social system networks, and large congregations are acknowledged
to be made up from multiple social networks in which individuals
and groups of individuals form subgroups or subconstituencies
within the congregation based on their personal passions, preferences, wants, and needs. For example, different and competing
constituencies may come to light during a budgeting process in
which the missions group might be in competition for dollars with

the group concerned about youth. Not as easily identifiable, there may be less formal subgroup constituencies in the congregation, such as the subgroup of members who prefer the associate clergy's warm personal and pastoral style over the senior clergy's clarity and officiousness. Commonly there will be a countersubgroup of members who prefer the senior clergy's clarity over the touchy-feely fuzziness of the associate. The point is that, formal or informal, large congregations come complete with multiple constituencies—all seeking to meet their purpose or preference. All staff in a congregation are formally or informally aligned with one or more of those constituencies—either by job description or relationship.

The need for clear alignment around central outcomes for ministry and the natural identification and representation of a subgroup constituency that is connected to the staff person's area of responsibility put each staff person in a natural tension. Staff members, including senior clergy, consistently must negotiate their path between a set of tensions that might be represented as follows:

Being the singular leader ←→ Being a team member
Being responsible for my work ←→ Being responsible for our mission
Being accountable to my constituency ←→ Being accountable to the senior clergy

As in all tensions, the truth is not to be found at one pole in opposition to the other. We all live in the middle of such tensions or polarities and are in constant negotiation with the opposing pulls that we feel. The staff meeting, however, is a place and time when a center can be felt, both poles easily can be identified, and efforts can be realigned appropriately. This can be seen more clearly if we identify the purposes and principles of staff meetings.

The Purposes of Staff Meetings

Following is a list of purposes that are addressed in staff meetings in large congregations. Every staff meeting may not intentionally touch all of these areas, but these purposes rest at the heart of forming a healthy team of called and employed staff for ministry.

Missional Alignment

The staff meeting is the place where the senior clergy can rehearse and remind others of the larger ministry of the congregation. As noted in chapter 6 on supervision, it is the visioning task of the senior clergy to bring clarity to the picture of the congregation's calling. This clarity might be advanced at a staff meeting through the intentional revisiting of mission and outcome documents developed by the board or staff. The clarity might be advanced as the senior clergy takes time in a staff meeting to report on what he or she is working on with the board as the future of the congregation continually is shaped. Clarity may be addressed by celebrating the work of one of the staff members or a group in the congregation who have taken a step to advance the mission. Clarity may be sharpened through questioning the proposal of one or more of the staff members to see how the proposed effort supports the congregation's mission. Clarity may be improved as the senior clergy challenges a staff member to eliminate a program, a practice, or a preference because it does not align with the mission.

While done in multiple ways, one of the central purposes of the staff meeting is to remember and rehearse the vision so that each staff person can find the way in which his or her "part" supports and deepens the mission of the "whole." Gordon Kingsley, former president of William Jewell College in Liberty, Missouri, described the central function of a leader as being the bard or poet who would "sing the song" of the organization so that others could learn the words and find their own place in the harmony.[1] The staff meeting provides the platform for this visioning work of the senior clergy because it is one of the few times when staff are all gathered together.

Developing Community

As noted, staff members in a large congregation are not commonly gathered in one place because their work is scattered over different areas in the facility and community, over different days and hours, and among different congregational and community constituencies. The fact that so much of the work of each individual staff member is done without significant overlap in place, time, or constituency lends to the temptation and perception of working alone. Staff members need a reminder that they are part of a community called to a shared purpose and that the mission of the congregation will not and cannot move ahead just with their own skills and efforts. We all need reminders of what others "bring to the table," as well as the reminder that we need to share our own gifts with others to move the ministry ahead. Being reminded that we are part of a community can be achieved as simply as having a time and a place to gather regularly to sip coffee together as a group, share prayer or singing, or even review the week's calendar. Seeing people's faces and remembering their presence—even if our work does not frequently cross paths with theirs—is nonetheless a powerful reminder of team and community.

Information Sharing: "No Surprises"

Staff meetings are principle times of sharing information. Every staff member does not need to, and should not expect to, know everything that all other staff are doing. Staff teams are not themselves accountable for the full ministry of the congregation. That is the task of the senior clergy and the board. Staff teams are not responsible for strategizing and shaping the work of each of the individual people who make up the team. To have everyone's work processed and agreed to by all other staff members is an exceedingly expensive use of time, an inappropriate use of human resources, and an organizationally constraining practice. Senior clergy must carefully steer staff meetings away from using group time to do one or two staff members' work or planning, which should more appropriately be done outside of the staff meeting.

The basic principle of information sharing that needs to be practiced is "no surprises." Everyone on staff does not need to know everything that others are doing. No one on staff, however, should be surprised to hear, generally, what is being done in the congregation and, specifically, what has been decided or planned that will have a direct impact on their own work and responsibility. The "no-surprise" criteria can be a helpful measure of what needs to be shared as information at a staff meeting. From one perspective, as Gil has learned to say after working for years with congregations around issues of conflict, "Surprised people behave badly." From an even more important perspective, "surprises" among or between staff team members may be evidence of the absence of alignment and coordination.

It is important for staff to recognize that information sharing and storytelling are not the same thing. It is our common experience that staff in large congregations frequently offer too much information because they want to tell—and have others hear—the "whole story." For example, everyone in a staff meeting does not need to hear why a particular member of the congregation is in the hospital, what tests have been done, and what her sister had to say about it. Staff members simply need to know that the person is in the hospital and that someone on staff has the responsibility to provide congregational contact and care. In other words, the purpose of sharing information is to prevent surprises and to align the work. Sharing information is not an invitation for others to review the work, raise questions about how a staff person is shaping the work, or suggest improvements—unless asked.

Supervision of Group Work

The supervision of an individual staff member was discussed in chapter 6. That supervisory conversation was approached from the perspective of being a learning time for the senior clergy and staff member to talk together about the work of the staff person. The conversation is to be formative, not summative. Remember, summative leads to a conclusion, an evaluation—is this person doing a good job?—while formative leads to learning and helping the person move ahead—what changes or resources would help this person advance his or her work and the mission of the congregation?

The staff meeting is an opportunity to invite the team to do group formative evaluation. While a formative conversation may not be on the agenda every time the team meets, the staff meeting nonetheless is an opportune—and often rare—moment to do the reflective work of formative evaluation. The senior clergy can introduce this group supervision by putting formative questions on the agenda, for example:

What have we been doing?
What are we learning about our work and our mission?
With whom do we need to build new or better relationships and coalitions to advance our work?
What should we be giving ourselves to with priority in the next week, month, and quarter?

A quarterly questions

Role Renegotiation

As work moves ahead, we all find that our job descriptions and assigned roles are necessarily malleable and need to be held loosely. For example, I may be hired as a youth program director, but to do my job and to support the work of the outreach and membership development coordinator, I will need to have contact with new members or may be needed to make contact with prospective members. My work as a youth staff member cannot be cordoned off in my own smaller world. Ministry in large, complex congregations demands great interplay and flexibility.

Corporations have long discovered that departments and workers that operate in silos—stand-alone units without connections to other departments or functions—reduce productivity and results. Organizations need clear but fluid boundaries so that departments, programs, and staff can function appropriately across silos to support the mission of the congregation. The staff meeting is a forum for discovering where boundaries need to be porous and where work must be collaborative rather than siloed. Staff naturally use staff meetings for negotiating inclusion or exclusion of others to strategize how to move work forward. It is the task of the senior clergy to moderate these conversations by continually asking who needs to be included in shared work as opposed to who may want to be or whom is asked to be included out of a sense of group loyalty. The staff meeting is an appropriate and natural place for this negotiation.

On a similar but less formal level, work patterns can be negotiated at staff meetings. Staff members can be invited to state their needs during staff meetings and thus clue others as to how they might appropriately offer support or reduce distractions. For example, when asked what information he needed from his staff, one senior clergy noted that he needed any and all information that would keep him from being surprised by a question from the board, but he added that he did not want copies of all e-mails sent to others or e-mails that only carried a "thank you" or "got it" response to an e-mail he had sent. Staff meetings are appropriate clearinghouses for such statements of need. "I need all worship bulletin information by Wednesday" or "I need to know who is in the building" or even "I need people to close their office doors in our cramped office suite when they are going to be on the telephone for an extended period of time." These are all appropriate requests that can be negotiated at a staff meeting.

Negotiating changes in one's role and work patterns is a critical but often difficult conversation for staff health and productivity. Our work, our role, and even our job descriptions grow and change over time as the work of the congregation develops. Add to this the reality that we all continually learn more about what we need as our work develops. Nonetheless, it is common for team members to resist stating their needs and negotiating these changes. While the staff meeting is a natural place for such conversations as a part of an appropriate meeting agenda, there are times in which the re-negotiation of role and needs must be more formally approached. (Refer back to chapter 8 for more on role renegotiation.)

Developing Staff (and Congregational) Culture

Every congregation has its own unique personality and culture. Walter Wink speaks of the "angel of the church"—the sense of both personality and vocation that reflects where a congregation has come from, where it is going, and what it is like to be within it.[2] Formal or informal, introverted or extroverted, valuing give-and-take as a team or deferring to the authority of certain leaders, valuing seriousness and insight or valuing play and creativity, expecting polite harmony or expecting statements of directness—every congregation is both guided and constrained by a silent and tacit set of norms that can either support or suppress ministry. The staff meeting is a place, a platform, where norms can be tested and changed as senior clergy work with their staff. If the congregation is constrained by a politeness and seriousness that do not invite people to engage one another, the senior pastor can develop norms of laughter and playfulness in the staff meeting to offer a counterbalance. Health comes from the center of an organization—by the healthy practices of the staff and volunteers who sit in the central positions of leaders. Staff and volunteer leaders actually model and mentor the rest of the congregation in appropriate ways of relating to one another, talking with one another, making decisions with each other, and a host of other critical but hidden norms that guide the life of the congregation. The staff meeting is a dominant and public place of gathering for a key group of congregational leaders. It is a platform from which new norms can be tried and modeled for the congregation and from which healthy practices of honesty and trust can be introduced into the larger body of the congregation.

Four Practices for Staff Meetings

Just as there are a number of purposes served by healthy staff meetings, there are also several practices that are both widely shared and experienced as productive for the life and work of the staff team. Below we identify four that are common in staffs with which we work.

Follow a Standard Format

A predictable format and dependable agenda for meetings will allow and instruct staff to share information and raise questions in

a helpful way. Knowing what to expect in an agenda for the staff
meeting allows the staff person to know how and when to contribute
his or her part to the work of the team.

Don't Rush to Decision Making

Staff meetings are not gatherings in which everyone must participate in every conversation, be involved in all decisions, and reach
unanimous agreement. Information sharing is not the same as
group decision making. Collaboration and alignment of effort are
not the same as approaching an issue or question as a "work of
the whole." Decisions belong to the persons or groups who have
authority and accountability for making something happen. Staff
meetings in which team is built and information is shared are still
good meetings—even if no decisions are made.

Delegate and Entrust

After information is shared at a staff meeting and issues and questions are identified, the staff members involved in and responsible
for a task should be invited to work "off-line" or outside of the
staff meeting where everyone's time and attention will not be taken
up by work that belongs to only one or a few. When the full staff
begins to do the work that belongs to only one or a few, the senior
clergy needs to ask that the conversation continue in the appropriate person's office after the staff meeting is adjourned. Sharing too
much information and doing too much "work as a whole" are major
causes of staff meetings that last beyond their productiveness.

Include the Right People at the Right Time

Staff meetings that last too long with too many people tied up and
away from their tasks are both the temptation and frustration of
many staff members. Support staff surely need to be at the table
when coffee and fruit are being shared and when people are being
reminded of their part in the team by looking others in the eye.
Support staff also need to be present at the table when the calendar

is reviewed so that they are not surprised by what mailings need to go out or what rooms need to be available. They, however, do not need to review all of the names of people needing pastoral care. Similarly, staff who have primary responsibility for pastoral care as their singular responsibility do not need to sit through a discussion of a new effort to train volunteers for youth ministry. Because all staff are not needed in every conversation, staff meetings tend to get smaller or larger as the meeting continues and as the agenda moves on to include fewer or more people. The staff meeting agenda can be built to begin with issues that belong to everyone, such as calendaring, and then move to issues belonging to smaller subgroups so that those not involved can return to their work. Examples of staff meetings will be shared below, specifically illustrating starting meetings with all staff (clergy, program, administrative, and support) present for community building. As the agenda moves on, some staff are invited to return to their work since only some of the staff with prescribed responsibilities need to remain in the meeting.

Other Issues

As noted above, every congregation has its own personality and style. So any guidelines or principles about shaping staff meetings must be held loosely; congregations need to be encouraged to adapt the meetings to their own setting. That being said, there are a number of issues that we note as being often-asked questions. While there are a wide variety of practices around these questions, we simply offer our own preferences and experiences about these topics.

How Long Should a Staff Meeting Last?

Ninety minutes seems to be a norm in many large congregations, a midpoint between the one-hour and two-hour meetings that tend to form the lower and higher boundaries practiced in congregations. The natural temptation of established institutions is to become internally focused and to use too much time and too many resources to "keep the wheels turning." The natural temptation of staff in congregations—who often come to their work with a deep sense of care and relationship—is to be in conversation and relationship beyond the needed limit. We encourage clear and predictable agendas with careful monitoring of the group's work by the leader as a way of having productive staff meetings that do not exceed expected time limits. If additional work must be done before the next meeting, it may be preferable to ask one or two of the staff members to work off-line so that everyone's time and attention are not captured beyond a productive limit.

Should Our Staff Meeting Include Worship, Study, and Play?

Surely it is appropriate for any staff meeting to include some element of worship, prayer, or play. As noted above, however, the staff meeting is a time of shaping and aligning the work of the congregation for the accomplishment of the mission. While a staff meeting might include a time of prayer or centering, it is not the time and place for a worship experience focusing on the spiritual lives of staff members. The same is true for study and play. While elements of study may be employed in a staff meeting as a basic idea is shared or elements of play are used as a brief exercise, the purpose of study is shared learning and the purpose of play is group and relational development. If learning or group development becomes the dominant agenda, another meeting at some time other than the staff meeting should be planned.

Are There Ways to Abbreviate the Routine Work Required in a Staff Meeting?

To keep pace with a demanding environment, many corporations and professionals are learning to outsource those parts of their work that are "fungible," or interchangeable, to others who can provide a service that does not need to come directly from the parent company or individual professional. For instance, some insurance claim processing for American insurance companies is outsourced to companies in Ireland so that the American companies are not slowed down by the time or cost of doing this work itself. While

a restaurant must surely have staff present to deliver the food and
service to the customer who obviously is present in the restaurant,
there are fungible pieces of the work that, when done by outside
workers, will allow for maximizing the attention and talents of those
who work with the customers. Some restaurant chains are experimenting with outsourcing customer reservations so that the staff at
the restaurant may give their complete attention to customers, meal
preparation, and service. It is possible for your phone reservation
to be taken by an "outsourcing company" located in India or some
other distant place and still have a table waiting when you arrive
at the restaurant. Congregational staff also can look for group
work that is fungible and develop ways to outsource the work to
an individual outside of the staff meeting. The goal is to reduce the
time, energy, and attention the full staff gives to tasks that can be
managed in other ways. Two simple examples follow:

Calendar review. To avoid prolonged discussion about the
calendar, staff can develop both tools and protocols to move them
through this conversation quickly. For instance, in one congregation everyone on staff was asked to give all calendar information
to the appropriate secretary by the close of the office the evening
before the meeting. The secretary then would prepare an updated
copy of the calendar for the next two weeks and distribute it to the
people at the staff meeting the following morning. The calendaring
conversation was to follow a protocol of two questions:

1. Is the calendar for the next two weeks correct and complete, or do we see any conflicts that need to be resolved
   following this meeting?
2. Is the calendar for the next three months correct, or are
   their additions that need to be made?

Of course, all staff received copies of the complete annual
calendar, which was updated regularly. Full calendars, however,
were not routinely reviewed by all staff members as a part of staff
meetings.

Pastoral care review. To avoid prolonged discussion and storytelling about those needing and receiving care from the staff,

pastoral care 13+

some congregations use an Excel spreadsheet to focus on the information necessary for staff to provide this care. The appropriate person—secretary or staff person responsible for coordinating pastoral care—distributes an updated report at the staff meeting. The conversation about pastoral care is managed by reviewing and updating the report. The sheet may look as follows:

Name	Location: Hospital or other	Beginning date of pastoral care	Staff person responsible for contact

The protocol for reviewing pastoral care may be a small set of standard questions, such as the following:

Who has been on or needs to be added to this list?
Who on staff has primary responsibility to provide contact and care?
Who is to be taken off the list?

Some discussion about individual situations is necessary and appropriate to determine the best manner of providing care. Staff meetings, however, are not the appropriate forum for telling stories and rehearsing the experience of providing care.

Should Part-Time Staff Be Required to Attend?

There are a number of tradeoffs in this question. The expectations and limits of the work of part-time staff in congregations often are set by an hour boundary, such as ten hours per week. Since this represents limited access to the resource that this person represents, some thought must be given to the value of using one to one and a half hours of that time for attendance at a staff meeting. However, it also must be noted that part-time staff frequently increase the supervisory responsibility of the senior clergy or another designated supervisor because they are not as closely connected to others and to the larger mission. More time commonly has to be given in the supervisory relationship to updating and aligning the effort of the part-time person to the life of the larger mission to which he or she does not have access. We have observed staffs take a variety of positions on this question of attendance, including the following:

- Part-time staff always are expected to attend staff meetings.
- Part-time staff never are expected to attend staff meetings.
- Part-time staff are expected to attend staff meetings only when their area of responsibility is on the agenda.
- Part time-staff are welcome to attend all staff meetings but are expected to be present only when their area of responsibility is on the agenda. (The invitation rather than a requirement to attend indicates that the time given to the staff meeting is offered by the staff person and is not counted toward the work time of that person.)

Some Examples of Staff Meetings

Below are three examples of staff meetings that we have observed in large congregations. You will note that they are similar but somewhat different based on the culture and preferred style of the congregation or the staff.

1. Informal

Less formal and more conversational, the informal staff meeting does not begin with a formal agenda but invites the agenda to develop as staff persons check in with their work.

Gathering. A time of prayer and a quick circle around the table to invite staff members to share any personal news.

Calendaring. A brief open conversation about the week ahead and any changes or additions to the calendar of the congregation.

Member care. A brief open conversation about the people receiving care or needing care and who is responsible to provide that care.

Agenda items. Each staff person is invited to take a turn to update others on his or her work, identify issues, or ask for feedback or help. (Note: It may be important to ask staff to prioritize quickly what needs to be discussed or at least to invite staff members who feel the most pressure on their reporting to go first. The risk of an informal agenda is to invite a form of "work avoidance"—saving the more difficult conversations until there is not enough time to work on them appropriately.)

2. Questions Format

In the questions format, the staff meeting follows a protocol of questions that essentially remain the same from one meeting to another. The fact that the questions do not change allows staff members to know how to get their information before others during a meeting. In one congregation where this format was followed, the questions were written on a whiteboard prior to the meeting, and every staff person was expected to post issues after any question where they needed group time. These notes were to be posted on the whiteboard prior to the start of the meeting. After an opening prayer, the senior pastor would assign a tentative timeline to the various questions based on the notes offered on the whiteboard so that the meeting would not run past the ninety-minute limit.

Gathering. Coffee, placing notes on the whiteboard, and opening prayer.

The protocol of questions.

- What do we need to check on the calendar for this week? This month?
- Who needs care?
- What information do you have that others need?
- What do you need to present to the team in order to get help or support?
- What "big picture" or future issue do we or our congregation need to be aware of?

Next steps. What needs to happen before our next meeting?

3. Selective Participation

In the selective participation format, the staff team leader carefully attends to who is in the room during the meeting so that people's time is not used inappropriately.

All staff. Clergy, program, administrative, and support staff.

- Coffee, conversation, and opening prayer
- Calendar review, using the two-week review process described earlier.
- Brief information sharing of items about which everyone needs to know.

Pastoral care. Clergy, program staff, and executive secretary.

- Reviewing the report for pastoral care using the Excel spreadsheet described earlier. In this congregation the responsibility for updating the pastoral care report belongs to the executive secretary, which explains her or his role in this part of the meeting.

Program team. Clergy and program staff.

- This part of the meeting is given to program review and is an opportune time for group supervision and formative evaluation.

Worship team. Only those clergy and program staff with worship responsibilities.

- In many congregations the worship team meets at a separate time apart from the staff meeting. When connected to the staff meeting, it is important to include only those who have responsibility for worship planning to participate. The final portion of the staff meeting by the worship team may, in fact, be a separate one-hour meeting that begins after a break from the staff meeting.

It should be clear from the above discussion that there are multiple ways to develop staff meetings. The style of the meeting must fit the style of the senior pastor and the culture of the congregation. However, whatever the style, the meeting must be purposeful and transparent—staff must be clear about what needs to be accomplished in the meeting and must be aware of a predictable agenda that allows each person to know how to participate effectively. Collaboration of efforts among staff and the opportunity to reflect together on how each person's work is aligned—or needs to be aligned—with the congregation's central mission are critical issues of effectiveness. The staff meeting is the key opportunity to work together on collaboration and alignment. It is an opportunity that must not be squandered.

Chapter 12

Dealing with Difficult Staff Behavior

"Once upon a time in the Friendly Forest there lived a lamb who loved to graze and frolic about. One day a tiger came to the forest. . . ."[1] So begins one of the pithy metaphorical stories about relationships written by rabbi, writer, and teacher of family systems theory Edwin Friedman. The story goes on to tell how the lamb wanted to accept the tiger as a forest mate but became increasingly nervous about its growling and menacing gestures. But everyone always wants others to get along, so when the lamb became upset, the other animals of the forest explained that growling was just the tiger's nature and should be ignored. The lamb became increasingly upset and even wanted to leave the forest but again was met by the other animals who counseled understanding and negotiation. It was just a matter of communication, the lamb was told. Everyone clearly was invested in keeping the relationships as they were and making them "work" until one wise and much more realistic animal finally proclaimed it all nonsense, saying, "If you want a lamb and a tiger to live in the same forest, you don't try to make them communicate. You cage the bloody tiger."

barnlani:

People who work and worship in congregations naturally want everyone to get along. The values of politeness and care for others are held high in faith communities, and these values at times can permit behaviors that are neither healthy nor helpful but are tolerated because "we all want everyone to get along." The reality is that when there is bad behavior in a congregation or staff team, someone needs to put boundaries around it. Bad behavior needs to be recognized as something more than "a communication problem," which is perhaps one of the most frequent presenting diagnoses that a consultant will hear from a leader who wants help with his or her staff team. Bad behavior needs to be caged.

Help in communication may very well be the need of the group. In chapter 8 the need to negotiate pinches felt between coworkers was addressed, and attention was given to helping people communicate their discomforts before they became disruptive to the working relationship. The leader, however, must distinguish between a need to help staff members provide additional information to make the work and the relationships move more smoothly and the need to bound behaviors that are unhealthy and unfaithful. When does it become clear that it is necessary to put a stop to some behavior because it is unhelpful? One of us received a call from a congregation asking for help in team building because the staff agreed that they needed to communicate better. There is always a story that goes along with every request for a consultation. In this case, the story centered around one long-tenured and dominant staff person who spoke more than listened; discounted or ignored the requests of others, including the senior clergy; and, when he did not get his way with his colleagues, talked openly to his subgroup of loyal supporters in the congregation about how he was "never listened to." It was clearly evident that the issue was not communication or improving relationships. This worker was practicing inappropriate and unhealthy behavior and needed to be stopped. The rest of the staff members were hoping that a consultant could come in and "fix" this guy. Clear boundaries were needed, and the bad behavior needed to be caged.

Bad Behavior vs. Appropriate Discomfort

It is vital for the leader to be aware of the difference between appropriate discomfort that comes from healthy disagreement about ideas and convictions and the disruptive discomfort that comes from losing trust in or feeling dismissed by a colleague. Congregations are network organizations that are heavily dependent upon and therefore sensitive to relationships. Ministry, in fact, is accomplished by using relationship as the very currency of exchange. Many clergy leaders have heard or told stories of the person who began as a leading opponent but then took a surprising turn to become a strong supporter. In one of these stories, a member of the congregation surprised everyone on the governing board by his uncharacteristic support of his pastor, explaining, "I stand with my pastor this evening because he stood with me at the hospital when my wife died."

Relationships play an unusually powerful role in congregations that is not mirrored in many other organizations and rarely mirrored in any other work setting. Our sensitivity to these relationships often has set us in search of a false harmony in which we believe that everyone must always agree and that it is inappropriate for anyone to be upset. We frequently work with congregational leaders who have exceptional skills that go unused or abandoned because the leader is "afraid of conflict" and too uncomfortable with the evidence of discomfort in others.

Discomfort and disagreement, however, are a natural and necessary stage in the development of a group that is moving toward honest creativity. It is the chaos that allows us to move past what Scott Peck, therapist and author who turned his attention to community building, describes as "pseudo community." Says Peck, "The first response of a group seeking to form a community is most often to try and fake it. The members attempt to be an instant community by being extremely pleasant with one another and avoiding all disagreement."[2] His conclusion about this false sense of harmony and agreement is that it never works.

The reality is that differences and disagreements about our work and our mission are more than natural; they are needed. Ronald Heifetz, whose work was cited in chapter 8, writes along with his colleague Donald Laurie, "Different people within the same organization bring different experiences, assumptions, values, beliefs, and habits to their work. This diversity is valuable because innovation and learning are the products of differences."[3] In other words, the disagreements and discomforts that come from our differences need to be preserved and managed. It can be helpful to realize that from a general systems theory approach, the innovation that comes from disagreement over ideas is a source of life for an organization. If there must always be agreement and no one in discord, there cannot be multiple ideas present in the system. Two or more ideas in the same place at the same time create friction. The only way to avoid that friction is to live with a single idea. An organization that can hold only one idea, however, can only do what it already has done. In a fast-changing environment, such as the communities and the culture that surround our congregations, doing only what we always have done is the kiss of death.

The conclusion, therefore, is that the leader needs perspective on what lies at the root of the discomfort being experienced within a staff. At this point we are talking about three different kinds, or causes, of discomfort about which staff members might feel anxious and want to escape or that are perceived as disruptive of work and relationships:

1. Discomfort that comes from knowing that others around the table disagree as we explore ideas, hunches, convictions, and preferences. In a changing environment that depends on the creativity of adaptation and invention, this discomfort is to be protected and preserved at all costs. Senior leaders need to provide the safety and guidance that keep people at the table and engaged in conversation that may feel uncomfortable so that new things can be learned. Knowledge management is now a developing discipline in many businesses because of the need for new ideas to match the new and fast-changing settings for our work. Quoting Alan Webber, business authors Thomas Davenport and Laurence Prusak highlight the critical importance of conversational give-and-take among workers. They note, "Conversations are the way knowledge workers discover what they know, share it with their colleagues, and in the process create new knowledge for the organization."[4] This discomfort is to be valued.

2. Discomfort that comes from not getting what is needed from coworkers—or, conversely, getting what is unneed-

ed. This is the discomfort—described in chapter 8—that comes when pinches are felt in working relationships between staff members. Again, these pinches are natural and normal. They stem from a changing environment that makes old agreements and practices less satisfying or from new behaviors by colleagues that were unexpected because insufficient information was present about their needs or preferences for doing their work. The appearance of such pinches is evidence of developing ministry since something has changed sufficiently to produce the unexpected. The point of chapter 8 is that these pinches are possible to negotiate before they become problems ("crunches"). It is the responsibility of the leader to create the safe space and model a willingness to discuss and negotiate these discomforts as a way of establishing a new stable platform from which the staff members can work with a sense of trust.

3. Discomfort from unhealthy behaviors that make it feel unsafe to be around the table with colleagues. It is this third type of discomfort—and the unhealthy or unhelpful behaviors that create it—that must be addressed directly by the senior leader alone or working with the whole staff team. How will we know it? Unhealthy, unhelpful behavior may appear as:

- Disagreements that are focused on the person rather than on the idea.
- A staff member's focus on himself or herself above and against the mission of the group.
- Turf protection and an unwillingness to give others information they need.
- Triangulating with others within or outside the staff as a strategy of opposition.
- A withholding of self and an unwillingness to get involved collaboratively with others.
- A practice of ascribing the worst rather than the best of motives to colleagues and the decisions they make.

- Sexist, racist, or other obviously inappropriate comments.

It seems as if unhealthy and unhelpful behaviors are both widely shared by many groups and, at the same time, unique in the way a particular person or group practices them. For those of us who work somewhat regularly with teams struggling with unhelpful behaviors, it can seem as though people try to be downright creative in finding ways to express such practices. How does the senior leader know if he or she is observing unhelpful behavior? The best response might be to trust the wisdom of John Guaspari, who amid the furor of trying to describe, define, and quantify "quality" in American manufacturing over the past two decades, wrote *I Know It When I See It: A Modern Fable about Quality*.[5] According to Guaspari, we will know bad behavior when we see it. Leaders need to trust their intuition.

Much of leadership is intuitive. Intuition may fly beneath our conscious radar, and we may not be able to explain—even to ourselves—what we know to be true or why we need to make a decision. Nonetheless, intuition is informed behavior; it is wisdom practiced at an earlier time and is available to guide us again because it was triggered by something familiar. In a creative time when much changes quickly, intuition needs to be both practiced and trusted. So how does the leader know if the discomfort should be protected or addressed? The leader needs to trust what he or she sees and feels:

- Is the discomfort engaging and producing new ideas or challenging past practices? Protect it, and encourage others to stay in the conversation.
- Is the discomfort a product of the group's development, of a changing circumstance in the work of the team, or of new needs by people to do their work well? Make it safe and provide a structured way for staff members to talk to one another about what they need more or less of.
- Is the discomfort the product of inappropriate behavior or practices that break relationships, trust, and information sharing? Cage it and install some controls.

Caging Bad Behavior

In his book on behavioral covenants, Gil wrote about resetting the defaults in a group or a congregation when inappropriate behavior is present.[6] Every group lives by established norms—the silent and hidden but very powerful "rules" by which we live and work. For example, a group may operate with a norm that a decision is never called for until the pastor already has indicated his or her preference about what should happen. One congregation might have a norm about information sharing in which everyone is aware that only the elected board members need to know all the details, while another congregation might have a norm in which it is expected that all members will be given all information before the board will deliberate. Many congregations operate with a norm that assumes that we never have any conflict, and when we do, we never talk about it openly. The group does not need to discuss these norms, and frequently people are not even aware of them. People just "know" that it works that way in a particular group because they have been given silent clues to support the norm or have received sanctions when they have not followed the norm.

Norms cover any number of issues, circumstances, or practices with previously established agreements and expectations so that a group does not need to stop at every point and decide again what is to be considered "normal" behavior. But these silent and hidden norms set the "default" by which the group will function. *Default* here is used in the same sense in which we apply this idea to computer software, such as a word processing program. When a new document is opened, the format already is set by established defaults for the margins, font, and spacing. Every time the user opens a new document, the same defaults will appear because they have been set as the norms.

In many ways the staff team—or even the whole congregation—has established defaults already installed by the surrounding culture that allow—or even at times encourage—less than helpful behavior. Because of the present culture of individualism, there is a rather broad range of behaviors that is accepted or tolerated in the American experience. Stephen Carter, professor of law at Yale University, has effectively described and helped explain the current cultural moment, which is marked by incivility and a lack of "an etiquette of democracy."[7] A culture and a time in which the individual is the final arbiter of what is right or wrong "for me" is also a moment in which behaviors that get "me" what "I want" are both accepted and rewarded. Municipal meetings or zoning board hearings are contentious times in which individuals or groups yell at each other because it is assumed that it is acceptable to "get what you want." Far too few congregations or faith communities of any kind make a distinction between behavior that is allowable or acceptable in the larger community and the different responsibility that we have for our behavior and our relationships with others in the congregation. Since unhealthy or unhelpful behavior is easily tolerated in a cultural time of incivility, such unhealthy or unhelpful behavior easily can slip into a congregation or staff team and be seen as "normal" by the practitioner. It may not occur to a staff member that it is inappropriate to talk to his subgroup of supporters in the congregation about a staff decision with which he disagreed and will not support because, after all, he or she is only being faithful to his or her own preferences or convictions. When we are accustomed to and rewarded for seeking our own benefit in the larger culture, it is more likely that selfish and unhelpful behavior also will slip into our work with one another in the congregation.

If there is to be a change in such behavior, new defaults need to be set. Without setting new standards, the old behaviors—the old "defaults"—consistently will reappear whenever the situation calls for them. The senior leader needs to take a role in setting appropriate boundaries by establishing new and healthy defaults—norms—of staff behavior.

Setting New Norms by Authority

Setting the norms of appropriate behavior is always within the authority of a leader. It is often an issue of <u>describing the unhelpful behavior, describing the more helpful behavior, and then making it clear that only the more helpful behavior will be accepted.</u>

In a business setting, a manager of a branch office of an insurance company replaced a long-tenured and well-loved predecessor who retired. As the new manager took office, a number of changes naturally were introduced—some as a consequence of the new manager's preference and some as an update of policies that had not been tended to by the former manager who thought things were fine as they were. Much grumbling among the workers ensued, and water cooler conversations about the good old days took up a considerable amount of time. After several weeks the new manager called a full-staff meeting and described to everyone what he had observed about the grumbling, the distracting conversations, and the resistance to changing practices of how the work would be done. He told the group that he understood how much and why they missed the former manager and that such behavior about the changes was very normal. He then informed everyone that he would accept this behavior for another week and then he would expect everyone to be on his team or else he would be willing to talk to people about moving to another team outside of their present position. It was a clear use of positional authority to reset the norms of the group.

Often in congregational settings positional power cannot be used quite so directly. The person in authority, however, can set limits and reset norms by controlling his or her own behaviors and indicating what he or she as leader is willing to accept and willing to do in response. For example, a middle judicatory executive was invited into a congregation that was in dispute with its pastor. People were behaving badly—not only with the pastor but with one another. The executive took careful notes on what he observed and then met with the governing board. Describing what he saw, he talked about the request for help these congregational leaders had given him. The executive then talked to the group about his expectations about their own behavior and told the group that if they expected him to help, he expected them to do the following:

- Stop participating in gossip about the minister and about each other.

- Pray daily for their pastor and for one another individually, by name, focusing especially on prayers for understanding and healing with the people with whom they most disagreed.
- Share any information that they had openly with the full board, paying attention to the difference between hearsay or rumor and what they knew to be fact.

The list went on a bit longer, but this leader's expectation was that if members of the congregation wanted his support, he expected their support in changed behavior. Rather than a demand from a position of authority, he used his leadership to negotiate by relationship.

At times the unhealthy behavior that needs to be addressed is practiced by only one individual rather than a full group, and the leader needs to address the issue one-on-one. The senior leader can use his or her authority to change the behavior or establish appropriate boundaries by giving that responsibility to the person who is behaving badly. For example, one senior pastor received a number of complaints from leaders that the executive minister who was responsible for financial reports did not produce the expected reports and that he was not willing to talk with them about changes that he made in the budgets for their areas of responsibility. The senior minister called the executive minister into his office and described the complaints, along with the names of the people who had offered the complaints. The senior pastor then said that he already had told each of the people offering a complaint that he would direct the executive minister to make an appointment to speak with them individually about their concern and report back to the senior pastor within a week with a plan to resolve the issues. The senior pastor then explained to the executive minister that he did not expect that the conversation would include anyone else on staff not involved in the complaints and that he would not accept any reprisals with the people who had shared complaints. Setting a date for the next meeting when the plan to resolve the issues would be discussed, the executive minister left with the appropriate "monkey" on his back (see chapter 6) with responsibility to reset his own behavioral norms in working with leaders.

Interesting case study

Setting New Norms with the Authority of the Group

There are times when the issue of appropriate and healthy behavior belongs to the full staff team. Healthy and faithful staff behavior is an appropriate and important topic for the full staff to work on as a group. This can be an important piece of work to do at some depth in a retreat setting when the staff members are invited to step away from the congregation and their work in order to take a dispassionate look at how they are doing. Gil has written material to help staff teams develop behavioral covenants:[8]

- A behavioral covenant is a written document developed by leaders, agreed to and owned by its creators, and practiced on a daily basis as a spiritual discipline.
- It is a covenant. It is not a set of rules; covenants refer to promises. While we currently live in a world of rules that are punishable when broken, promises are vows made with the intention of keeping them. The appropriate response to an unfulfilled promise is not punishment but further conversation about why the promise was hard to fulfill and what is appropriate to do next to honor each other.
- It is behavioral. It seeks to identify and negotiate changes in behaviors, not in personalities or values. One of the basic learnings of conflict management is that some things are negotiable while some things are not. Behavior is negotiable; personality is not.

While the operating norms of a staff often are hidden and tacit—flying below the screen of consciousness—it is not difficult to help surface the group's behavior for observation and evaluation. Gil's book on behavioral covenants has a number of models for doing such work in retreats, as well as in regular staff meetings. Work on behavioral covenants can bring clarity about behaviors that need to be tended and new norms that need to be practiced. Consider the clarity in the following example that was developed by the staff members of a large congregation during a time of great stress when unhelpful behaviors were being practiced widely.

Behavioral Covenant for the Staff
of _____ Church[9]

- We promise to value our ministry of leadership to our congregation as a team and to offer our primary loyalty to that team.
- We promise to express criticism and negative feelings first to the person, not to others.
- We promise to refuse to talk with a complainer until that person addresses the person she or he is complaining about.
- We promise to maintain confidentiality in staff conversations and meetings.
- We promise to explain clearly to people who bring staff complaints that we will be sharing the conversation with staff.
- We promise to commit to processing information about personality differences among staff and to give feedback to one another in order to support strengths and to balance weaknesses.
- We promise to openly discuss our personal strategies and investments in proposals being made.
- We promise to accept the fact that disagreements are expected and are to take place behind closed staff doors; in public we present ourselves as a team.

In many settings the promises that the staff members in the above example were making to one another would be assumed as standard practice and obvious to professionals. Whether the covenant focuses on obviously unhealthy behavior experienced in a difficult time or seeks to claim healthy and faithful behavior in a productive time of wanting to live out the mission of the congregation, changing the default by explicitly naming behaviors is a very powerful tool for leadership.

Modeling Healthy and Faithful
Behavior for the Congregation

As early as the 1980s, Ken Mitchell, family therapist and pastoral counselor, was applying systems dynamics to his experience of congregations. In his work on multiple staffs, he recognized that the relationships the staff maintain within itself are actually a model for the rest of the congregation and will set the norms—the standards—for others to follow, as well. Mitchell wrote, "When a subsystem takes leadership in a larger system, the smaller system's management of relationships is likely to be taken by members of the larger system as the norm for relationships."[10] Healthy staff behaviors are a tool of congregational ministry. One of the primary leverage points that a staff has to create a viable and healthy community within the congregation is their own behavior, which is observable and serves as a model for the way in which others will respond. The norms set within the staff can set or reset the norms in the congregation.

This is clearly seen through the behavioral covenant example above. In the example above, once the staff developed their promises to one another, their next step was to share their covenant with members of the governing board. In effect the staff was saying to the board, "This is how we have agreed to live and behave with one another as members of your staff." Having done that, the staff then asked for help and support from the board members. In other words, they were saying that, as staff members, they would not talk to a complainer about someone else on staff until that person had addressed the other staff member directly. The board members were being put on notice that they should not complain about one staff member to another staff member without taking the complaint where it belonged.

Whether it comes as an explicit request for members of the congregation to behave in appropriate ways or by observation of the actual behavior of the staff members, healthy behavior at the center of the congregation spreads outward into the larger congregation.

The dilemma is that unhealthy behavior at the center among staff also flows out into the larger congregation. It is the senior leader's responsibility to put boundaries around bad behavior so that what is modeled for others undergirds the building of healthy community.

Chapter 13

Dealing with Poor Performance or Terminating Employment

Actress Anne Bancroft was married to comedian Mel Brooks—a marriage many thought unlikely because of their remarkable differences. In one of the many interviews about their marriage, Bancroft said: "First of all you have to marry the right person. If you marry the wrong person for the wrong reasons, then no matter how hard you work, it's never going to work, because then you have to completely change yourself, completely change them, completely—by that time, you're both dead. So I think you have to marry for the right reasons, and marry the right person."[1]

That these two people found the "right person" in each other surprised many, which is a testament to the difficulty of seeing inside another's relationship. But the value of the right person in the right spot is equally important in the workplace. Not having the right person and committing to changing oneself or the other person as a way of making the relationship and the job "work" is a long-term and inadvisable strategy that may not lead to death but surely will feel like it.

Author Jim Collins, who studied companies and their leaders who were able to make the jump from mediocrity to excellence, advises that when staffing an organization, it is more important to find the right people first—even before setting the right outcomes. With the best mission and clear outcomes but the wrong people, it is unlikely that you will be effective. With the right people in place, however, the mission and the faithful outcomes will emerge. Using the metaphor of a bus, Collins writes, "The executives who ignited the transformations from good to great did not first figure out where to drive the bus and then get the people to take it there. No, they first got the right people on the bus (and the wrong people off the bus) and then figured out where to drive it."[2]

Getting the right people on the bus from the very beginning is an easier task in an upstart organization. Its importance can be seen in the deliberation and detail given by a newly elected U.S. president to forming the White House and national leadership teams immediately after the election—well before taking office in the new year. But most leaders—and most senior clergy in congregations—do not have the luxury of an upstart beginning. They inherit not only a staff, but also a mission, established outcomes, and practices. It is possible for a senior clergy to discover that he or she has inherited the wrong person in a position or that, as the mission and the identified outcomes for ministry change, the once right person no longer performs as well or as willingly as needed. As important as it is to get the right people on the bus, Collins also advises getting the wrong people off of the bus.

There should be no surprise that relationship-based organizations like congregations have a tendency to keep the wrong person in place too long. When bumps are discovered and work is not being done, many senior clergy and personnel committees respond with nurture and concern for the ill-performing worker. The stewardship question of whether the resource for ministry that this person represents is able to be used wisely and faithfully for ministry frequently is avoided. It is not difficult to find congregations that pay for personal therapy or provide funds for continuing education and training for an underperforming staff person with the hope of bringing that person to just the most basic level of performance—even though what is needed is impassioned, excellent leadership. Indeed, working to bring ill-prepared and poorly skilled candidates for ordained ministry up to the lowest acceptable standards is a trap in which many denominations find themselves, despite the awareness that it would be much more faithful to direct their resources and attention to inviting and calling the right candidates through active recruitment.

There is that moment, however, when the senior leader will find himself or herself wondering if the right person is on the bus—if the right staff person has been called to provide the leadership needed for the congregation. As we move into the issues of dealing with poor performance or terminating a staff person, we necessarily will pay attention to the issue of justice and fairness to the staff person. Wisely, addressing poor performance and terminating an employee should never be a precipitous move. Yet leaders need to pay attention to the measure of disappointment in a staff person's performance that would trigger the question of the appropriateness of the person remaining in the current position. Senior clergy often wonder when it is appropriate to begin to address poor performance and exiting. The answers, once again, are more intuitive than quantifiable. The senior leader must pay attention to and honor his or her own intuition and personal experience as a valid way to raise the issue. One of the most helpful triggers is identified by Collins: "The moment you feel the need to tightly manage someone, you've made a hiring mistake. The best people don't need to be managed. Guided, taught, led—yes. But not tightly managed."[3] Another trigger is the realization that the senior leader has been covering the same agenda of issues, expectations, and outcomes with the staff person, but there has been no appreciable movement toward the needed goals. Senior leaders are helped by paying attention to a feeling of dread or a weightiness when having to meet again with the staff member to try to motivate or direct that person toward needed performance. One of the questions a senior leader can monitor internally is whether he or she would feel a sense of relief or distress if that staff person came to share the news that he or she was leaving to take a position elsewhere.

Such intuitive measures and responses do not mean that the senior leader moves directly to termination. Any of these intuitions, however, indicate that it is appropriate for the senior leader to begin to think more formally about giving the staff person direct feedback and clear expectations about his or her work with an indication that the issue of continued employment or call is in question. It is time to move to the steps of progressive discipline as a way of providing more focused performance management for the staff person.

Steps of Progressive Discipline[4]

There are five steps in progressive discipline that are a part of a comprehensive plan of performance management of staff. The steps are meant to give careful feedback to a staff person about his or her performance and identify the issues of concern so that the staff person has both information and time to address the situation. It is not helpful to have any surprises when dealing with the staff person, and fairness requires that the person be offered both full information and sufficient time to make indicated changes. The five steps are as follows:

1. *The verbal warning.* The senior leader puts together a "talking paper" to use as a guide for a formal verbal conversation with the staff member after other, less formal discussions and performance reviews have failed to result in improved performance. Although the staff person should see that the senior clergy is referring to written notes, he or she should not be given a copy of the notes. It is important for the senior clergy to follow the talking paper closely and to keep any related follow-up notes from this meeting in the staff person's file.

2. *The written warning.* This document elevates the matter to a formal, documented process with specific provisions and timelines. It is commonly written by the chairperson of the committee responsible for employment and employees and is delivered by that person with another witness in the room. Sometimes a written warning is called a "probation." This is usually the longest, most detailed document in the progressive discipline process since it is meant to give clear and specific feedback on the behaviors or issues of performance in question. This document commonly is signed by both the senior clergy and the staff person at the end of the meeting in which it is presented to the staff person. It is common for the document to be written by the chairperson of the personnel committee or the board responsible for staffing the congregation. The

person who writes the document and the supervisor of the staff person sit together to talk with that person.

3. *The final warning.* This document also most normally is written by the personnel committee or the board—as appropriate by the polity or bylaws governing the congregation—based on the input of the senior clergy about the staff member's adherence to the provision of the written warning. Sometimes a final warning is called a "last-chance warning." This document is shorter than the written warning since it documents the reason(s) for issuing the final warning and then merely refers to the provisions within the written warning without repeating each of them. It is signed by the staff person and the appropriate representative of the personnel committee or board.

4. *The termination.* This document almost always is written by the personnel committee chairperson or board chairperson based on the decision to terminate the staff person. It is usually the shortest of all of the progressive discipline documents. The termination letter is written to the employee, and he or she does not sign it.

5. *The resignation agreement and general release.* While this document is not needed in every situation, it sometimes is appropriate to execute this document—particularly if there is the potential for legal exposure or repercussions in the congregation. This document can be quite lengthy, and the writer may need legal assistance. The resignation agreement states the terms and expectations of the termination, as well as what will be publicly announced by both the board and the departing staff member. When a full resignation agreement and general release are not required, a shorter "severance agreement" may be used.

An Example

Following is an example that uses the first steps of progressive discipline and is meant to give the reader a sense of the progression of these conversations and the documents that accompany them. The fifth step that includes a resignation agreement and general release may or may not be needed; if needed, it is clearly specific to the situation. In all steps, care must be taken to follow denominational polity and congregational bylaws. Consultation with an attorney may be advisable if there is evidence that the steps are leading to termination and there are questions of compliance with federal or state employment laws.

The Situation

Peter is an associate pastor of a congregation of fourteen hundred members. He is one of three full-time ordained clergy on staff, including the senior clergy, and he has supervisory responsibility for three program directors and the youth minister. He has held his position for eleven years—eight of which were spent working with a former senior pastor who had a conversational style of supervision with few clearly identified outcomes and expectations for the work of the staff members he supervised. For that eight-year period, Peter felt free to set his own goals and monitor his own work. For the past three years, Peter has been working with Ben, the new senior clergy who has a very different style than his predecessor.

Ben was very intentional in his first year as senior clergy to learn the call and gifts of this congregation and staff. By the end of his second year, Ben led the board into a full articulation of the mission of the congregation and the outcomes toward which the staff and leaders would work to be faithful to the mission. Ben very carefully included the staff in the conversation about the shaping of the new mission through the regular staff meetings so that no one on staff would be surprised by changes in priorities as new outcomes were identified.

As Ben began to share how the new missional outcomes would impact the work of the individual staff members through one-on-one meetings with each program staff member, it was clear to Peter that his job description and style of leadership with others was expected to change. The changes in outcomes and expectations of his work were uncomfortable for Peter, who inappropriately complained to a small group of members in the congregation whom he felt to be his supporters. Because his tenure at this congregation greatly exceeded

Ben's tenure as the senior clergy, Peter did not feel that changes in his work were either needed or appropriate, and he did not have any personal expectation that he should change the way in which he supervised others who reported to him.

Over the previous nine months, Ben had been very careful in visioning with Peter—both individually and in staff meetings—to be clear about what was expected and why it was important. Ben initiated a meeting with Peter—and all other clergy and program directors—to talk about changes in job descriptions and to make himself available for questions about the newly articulated mission of the congregation. Peter and Ben have had four performance management meetings focused on Peter's work in which Peter had not complied with the request by Ben for written pre-meeting notes. Ben also has received a number of complaints or concerns from the staff members whom Peter is to supervise about Peter's unavailability and unhelpfulness. Ben has learned that Peter resists setting supervisory meetings with others and that he does not inquire about their work or the resources they need for their work.

The Verbal Warning

Ben asked Peter to meet with him for a special session to review Peter's work. Prior to the meeting, Ben prepared a "talking paper"—a written document that he used very carefully in the conversation in order to be both accurate and transparent with Peter. He allowed Peter to see that he was working from a prepared document. He did not invite Peter to discuss or debate any of the points but instead asked Peter to listen without interruption so that Ben could be complete and clear about all he had to say. A copy of the talking points was not given to Peter. In this case, Ben decided that it was important to ask the personnel committee chairperson, Anne, to sit in on the meeting as an observer.

It may be helpful to note that we are now entering an area of supervision that many senior clergy and congregational leaders might feel to be countercultural to the normal practices of congregations because the feedback in a verbal warning is given very directly without careful considered attention to the emotional reaction that it might create in the staff member being warned. It is important to remember that a verbal warning over professional performance is not designed to provide professional or pastoral care to the staff member. Rather, the warning is focused in its feedback in order to convey the seriousness of the situation and to provide information on the specific attitudes and behaviors that the staff member will need to address to improve performance. While unusual in many congregations, such comprehensible and specific feedback to a staff member who is performing poorly is an issue of justice. The staff person needs clear information about what he or she must deal with. If the staff person values the position and feels clearly called to continue, there is information in this warning that will allow the staff person to make the necessary changes. If the staff person is underperforming or poorly performing because he or she is the wrong person for the position or because the sense of call to this work has diminished, it is a matter of justice for the senior pastor and personnel chairperson to give feedback that will help the staff person move on and not spend more time in a position that is neither good for the church nor for the staff person.

In the conversation with Peter, the talking paper had the following points:

- Thank Peter for coming.
- The primary purpose for this meeting is to set out my [Ben's] expectations for you in the coming year and to discuss your past performance in order to begin a dialogue between us.
- There are several areas where you have in the past exhibited and continue to exhibit outstanding performance:

  — Creativity in adult education planning.
  — Teaching the spring and fall biblical series.
  — Small group leadership training.

- Your performance in these areas has served the church well and is appreciated.

- There are, however, several areas of concern that are also your responsibility and need improvement:

> — Supervision of the three program directors and the youth minister.
> — Preparation for and participation in our performance management meetings as an opportunity for you to share information about your work with me.
> — Lack of full information sharing with other staff, including calendar planning with the support staff.
> — Sharing of your complaints about changes in your responsibilities with the group of members of the congregation with whom you have close personal ties.

- It is important for you to know that three of the four people for whom you have supervisory responsibility have spoken to me about your unavailability and your unwillingness to set supervisory meetings, saying instead that you have an "open-door policy" and they only need to stop by when they have a question. Both I and the chairperson of the board also have received several calls and complaints from members of the church who are very active with programs that you lead, wondering if you are being treated fairly and sharing complaints that you have talked with them about. I want to be clear that you have not shared those concerns and complaints with me.
- I have particular concern for the support and resourcing of our youth minister. As you know, this is the third youth minister our church has had in five years. This is a difficult position, and our present youth minister needs ongoing supervision and support.
- All of this is to say that there are several areas of your work that need serious attention and appropriate professional behavior. I have several recommendations for you to consider to make the needed improvements:

> — Begin to conduct regular meetings with the staff who report to you in order to provide the support and resourcing they need. You will have to learn more about what they are working on and what resources

they require to do their work. I recommend that you begin with weekly meetings until you and they feel that sufficient information has been shared. Begin with reviewing their new job descriptions and the outcomes that they are responsible for.

— Identify and use a book or a continuing education event that will help you to understand and improve in your supervisory responsibility. You are free to identify your own resource for this, but I am happy to make suggestions, and you will find our chairperson of personnel, who is a human resources director, very helpful.

- Beginning immediately, I would like to have weekly meetings with you in which we will discuss the status and activities of all of the work in your areas of responsibility. I also expect you to be prepared to share with me any concerns that you have about changes in your job description or responsibilities as we realign our work to fulfill the new mission of the church.

- I hope that we do not need to have further conversation about the inappropriateness of your talking to members of the church or other staff members with complaints about your work.

- [Pause] Question to Peter: Are there reasons that I should hear that can help me to understand these issues about your work? [Peter is given an opportunity to respond to the question.]

- My guess is that what I said today is difficult to hear. I understand that, but I believe that it is necessary to be open and candid with you for the sake of our church, and I want to build a strong working relationship with you.

- After taking time to come to grips with the seriousness of the situation, I would like you to reflect on what we have talked about today and come back to talk about how you intend to improve. Your reaction to this meeting is very important. I expect you to conduct yourself in a professional manner with renewed commitment and enthusiasm to your work and the people with whom you work. If you feel you need time off to do this, I welcome your request to do so.

- Remember, this meeting is confidential. Please do not leave this meeting and confront or inappropriately confide in others about what we have talked about here.
- Thank you for sitting through this and agreeing to work on these issues. This concludes our meeting.

Following the meeting, Ben made careful notes on Peter's response, any new information that Peter may have offered to explain his performance, and any commitments Peter made to address the issues identified in the conversation. The notes were dated and placed in Peter's file.

The Written Warning

Peter did meet weekly with Ben following the verbal warning. But resistance was notable in Peter's unwillingness to read a book or identify a continuing education event to help him with his supervisory role. While there were initial meetings between Peter and the four people whom he supervised, Ben discovered that there had been no follow-up. Peter had reverted to his "open-door" policy in which the burdens of getting support, resourcing, and accountability were placed back on the others. Most disconcerting was the clear evidence of Peter's continued complaining to members of the congregation about his "unfair" treatment by the senior clergy. In fact, the chairperson of the board received five complaints from members about Ben's leadership style, in which each of the individuals explained that they received their information in conversations with Peter.

While neither the board chairperson nor members of the personnel committee sat with Ben, Anne, and Peter for the verbal warning, these leaders were aware of the issues with Peter's work from reports Ben shared with them about his own supervisory work with staff. The personnel committee knew about and had approved the verbal warning and had received a subsequent report from Ben about that meeting. As Ben met with the personnel committee, they agreed that a written warning would be given to Peter and be written by Anne, the personnel committee chairperson. They also agreed that Anne would present the warning to Peter with Ben present as a witness. Peter was asked to meet with Anne and Ben after the warning was written, and Anne carefully walked Peter through the document by reading it aloud to be sure that all points had been made. The document follows:

Confidential Memo

To: Peter Brightham
From: Anne Winter, Chairperson of Personnel
Date: August 12, 2007
Re: Performance-Based Warning

After discussion with your supervisor, Rev. Ben Waters, it has been determined by the personnel committee that you are placed under a performance-based warning effectively immediately.

During your meeting with Rev. Waters on April 6, 2007, concerns regarding your performance were reviewed and you were provided with specific suggestions for improving your performance and professional behavior. Although you made initial efforts to implement some of the suggestions, you have not continued to follow through on them, and as a result, no noticeable improvement has been made.

The performance concerns discussed on April 6 are of a serious nature, particularly because of your role as associate pastor in our congregation. They are summarized as follows:

- Lack of consistent and ongoing supervisory meetings and the absence of support and resourcing needed by the persons for whom you have direct supervisory responsibilities.
- Lack of preparation for supervisory meetings with Rev. Waters, leading to a lack of transparency of your work and a perceived resistance to alignment of your work with the developing mission of our church.

- Lack of sufficient sharing of information about your work with your colleagues so that others are both aware of and able to coordinate with the programs that you lead.
- Continued unprofessional behavior of complaining to third parties who are congregational members and personal supporters of yours without addressing your concerns with Rev. Waters, your colleagues on staff, or the personnel committee.

These behaviors are inappropriate to a professional staff person and a spiritual leader in our community. Over the past four months, Rev. Waters has met with you regularly to update you on his assessment of your performance and to offer support for changes that you indicated you would make.

It is important for you to understand that these performance concerns are not items that are open to further debate or that you may dispute, but rather are a reiteration of the issues that Rev. Waters discussed with you in April.

Your position is in jeopardy.

The provisions of this performance-based probation are as follows:

- This warning is effective immediately, and you will remain under such warning until November 15, 2007. The personnel committee may determine that the warning be extended past this date or that other disciplinary action be taken. The expiration of the warning period should not be construed as any guarantee of continued employment by the church.
- Beginning immediately you will conduct weekly supervisory meetings and quarterly performance management meetings with the four persons for whom you have supervisory responsibilities. You must provide Rev. Waters a weekly written report of the information discussed in each of these meetings and review it with him, along with any pertinent information about your own work, on a weekly basis.
- You will register for and attend the Abbott System's one-day workshop on workplace supervision to be held at the

Hyatt Hotel on September 14, 2007. A written report of that workshop and what you learned as a participant will be given to me as chairperson of the personnel committee.

- Beginning immediately you will conduct yourself in a professional manner at all times and will address your concerns to your supervisor, Rev. Waters, or to me as chairperson of the personnel committee. The provisions of this probation are confidential, and under no circumstances are you to offer information about this probation or complaints about your treatment to members of the congregation or to your other colleagues on staff.
- You must improve your performance in each of the noted areas to at least a satisfactory level on or before the end of this warning. Determination of satisfactory performance lies solely with the personnel committee.

It is important to note that your reaction to this warning will be a determining factor of whether you will be allowed to continue your ministry as a member of the staff of this church. The personnel committee has the right to recommend the termination of your employment during this period if it is apparent that sufficient progress is not being made in regard to the provisions outlined in this warning.

We expect a heightened sense of commitment and enthusiasm from you in your daily activities, in dealing with the members of our congregation, and particularly with your direct reports and your supervisor, Rev. Waters. We expect that you will respond to this warning in a professional manner with no retaliatory actions taken against any other person.

At the conclusion of this probation, one of three actions will be taken:

1. You will return to regular employment status.
2. The warning will be extended under a final warning.
3. You will be terminated from employment.

It is my hope, as well as Rev. Waters's, that you will be able to improve your performance to a satisfactory level so that we will then be able to continue your relationship with our congregation as associate pastor.

PLEASE SIGN BELOW TO SIGNIFY THAT YOU HAVE READ, UNDERSTAND, AND AGREE TO THE PROVISIONS OF THIS PERFORMANCE-BASED WARNING.

_____   _____
Rev. Peter Brightham   Date

_____   _____
Anne Winter, Personnel Chairperson   Date

Note: If the staff person refuses to sign the warning, it is not necessary to try to coerce him or her into doing so. Simply write, "Employee refused to sign," on the employee's signature line, indicating that it was reviewed with the employee but that he or she declined to sign. This should be done in the presence of the employee and the other person who serves as a witness, and the employee should receive a copy of the document with the notation.

The Final Warning

The final warning (or third formal meeting) also is handled through a confidential memo that is shared with the employee by at least two persons, one of whom is the employee's supervisor. The final warning is a memo that identifies the action taken as a result of the probation described in the written warning above. It may be a notice of reinstatement to employment because of compliance with the provisions of the warning. It may be an extension of the timeline and requirements of the written warning above. Or it may be the delivery of notice of termination below. The purpose of this meeting is to give the employee the decision about next steps, using a written document that is read to the employee and, in the case of an extended final warning, to be signed by the employee for his or her file.

The Termination

Terminations of employees in congregations are commonly guided by the polity of the denomination or the bylaws of the congregation. These practices must be followed carefully and faithfully. In this fourth meeting, the employee should be given a written document indicating the process to be followed to termination and the decision of the personnel committee or appropriate office to follow that process. It is appropriate to discuss with the employee the options that he or she may have in ending the relationship through resignation or another means that is acceptable by denominational polity or congregational practice.

Concluding Notes

Congregations often find it difficult to terminate employees or to follow such formal practices of warnings and probations as described above. What is offered above is not meant to be a standardized template of the process and documents that must be used. This discussion of dealing with poor performance and termination, however, does seek to offer some tools and strategies for such serious and difficult conversations that give feedback, provide direction for remediation, and insist on accountability with the persons who are employed to serve the congregation and its mission. The level of formality and the actual process followed must be consistent with the culture of the congregation and the requirements of polity and bylaws.

Not to address poor performance, however, is an injustice to the person who is performing poorly, to his or her colleagues who must compensate or be limited by that person's poor performance, and to the mission of the congregation. Trying to nurture a staff person through a job for which he or she is not gifted or prepared is a disservice to that person whose gifts and life would be better spent in another congregation or position for which he or she is both fit and called. It is not uncommon for a person to look back over his or her work history and give thanks that at some point along the way a supervisor was courageous enough to give honest feedback about how the person did not fit the job or the job did not fit the person. Such feedback is commonly withheld because the supervisor is uncomfortable with conflict or uncomfortable with difficult feelings. Not addressing poor performance, however, means that the person will continue in a job or role that is inappropriate to his or her spirit or capacity. Since we are called to ministry to use our gifts and follow our passions, it is only just for the supervisor to point to where gifts and passions are missing or misspent so that the staff member can make appropriate changes in performance or seek a new job where gifts and passion can find freedom.

Chapter 14

Disclosure in Difficult Employment Situations

Recently All Saints Church fired a long-tenured staff member for lack of performance. Audrey had served All Saints for eight years as youth music director. Generally speaking, the youth liked being with Audrey. She was fun loving and energetic and always came up with new ways to engage the kids in the musical life of the congregation. Nevertheless, trouble with Audrey had been brewing for several years. Audrey failed to take direction from the music director and/or the senior pastor. She wasn't typically outright insubordinate but often passive-aggressively ignored directions given by her supervisors. Audrey had stopped attending weekly staff meetings several months prior to her dismissal, even though the meetings were mandatory for all employees. Audrey had also showed favoritism toward some of the youth in the congregation at the expense of other youth. Her pet favorites often got preferential treatment in the assignment of singing parts, and her pets were rarely the best musicians in the group. Audrey also exhibited poor judgment when it came to disciplining the kids. The senior pastor had received many complaints by maintenance workers about the condition of the choir room when Audrey's kids were done and occasional complaints from others about disrespectful behavior on the part of youth toward adult choir members. The event that ultimately resulted in Audrey's dismissal involved several of the youth swinging dangerously from a second floor fire exit during an evening choir practice that Audrey was supervising. No one was hurt in the incident.

Since her dismissal, Audrey has been "working" her relationships in the church to cause trouble behind the scenes. She is continually in contact with the families of her favored kids and has managed to get a number of those families to begin a movement to oust the music director. A growing number of congregation members are up in arms over Audrey's dismissal. Few families were aware of the problems Audrey had caused. The majority of the congregation had little contact with Audrey, but what little interaction they did have with her they liked. As time passes there is a growing sense of concern that Audrey was unfairly dismissed.

Attorneys advising the governing board at All Saints have urged congregational leaders not to discuss this issue with congregational members. They are concerned about potential legal liabilities that could occur if leaders begin talking about what Audrey did wrong or how congregational leaders responded. However, many people are beginning to challenge the decision that was made to fire Audrey, and the inability to talk about the situation is making things worse. What should congregational leaders do to manage the congregation's anxiety?

Let's begin by acknowledging that lawyers are doing their job well when they instruct congregation leaders not to talk about employee dismissal. An attorney is trying to protect the legal interest of the congregation by discouraging sidebar conversations that could be referenced later in a court of law. However, the legal needs of the congregation are only one set of needs to be considered at a time like this. Congregational leaders must also consider the need that members have to trust the actions of their leaders, the need of the community to act with personal and communal integrity, and the need of the community to care for members of the staff team, all of which are crucial in sustaining congregational health. Leaders must carefully consider ways in which they can talk about an employee dismissal that will minimize the risk of legal exposure but satisfy the community's need to know that their leaders have acted appropriately on their behalf.

The key to negotiating the murky waters of staff dismissal is to understand the difference between maintaining confidentiality and keeping a secret. We are keeping secrets from one another when we indicate that we know something others don't know and then refuse to talk about it. We are keeping secrets when we fail to tell people crucial information that they have a right to know. Secret keeping builds mistrust and creates barriers within a faith community. In the presence of secrets, people are painfully aware that something is going on that they know nothing about. Anxiety levels rise. As people become anxious, they look for information to settle their anxiety. In the absence of information, they begin to speculate and make up their own information, and the information they make up is almost always worse than reality.

Confidentiality, on the other hand, appreciates that some things should not become communally known. Confidentiality acknowledges that it is often in the best interest of persons and/or the congregation to protect specific facts that might be hurtful, misunderstood, or misused if shared. When congregational leaders treat employee dismissal information confidentially, they find ways to talk about the employee dismissal that protects the reputation of the employee and minimizes the legal risk to the congregation but satisfies the congregation's need to know that their leaders have acted appropriately and ethically.

Let's examine a few simple guidelines that allow congregational leaders to treat employee dismissals confidentially without creating a culture of secret keeping and mistrust.

Talk about process, not about content. Assuming that congregational leaders handled the employee's dismissal appropriately, we can also assume that a process was followed to examine the charges against the employee and to engage a disciplinary process leading up to termination. Congregational leaders can talk openly about the congregation's progressive discipline policy, assuring congregational members that these steps were followed in this particular case. Leaders should treat all information about the specific behaviors of this employee confidentially. The congregation has a need to know that its process operated with integrity. Although members may like to know the specific details of the situation, they do not have a need to know these details. They do have a need to know that their leaders acted with fairness and integrity.

Oftentimes leaders are afraid to talk openly about the process that was engaged, because they are aware that some mistakes were made along the way on the part of leadership. Such was the case with

Audrey. The music director had let Audrey's bad behavior go for so long that when he finally did decide to act, he didn't have all of the needed documentation to demonstrate that a series of performance conversations had taken place. However, board leadership had been involved in the decision, and all agreed that the dangerous incident with the youth on the fire escape overrode the policy requirements for a lengthier dismissal process.

Although a purely legal approach may not endorse open acknowledgment of error, it is important to own any mistakes that may have occurred in executing a disciplinary process. If you find yourself in such a situation, talk openly about your regret over those mistakes, and explain the corrective actions taken to mitigate those errors. A congregation is a covenantal community that requires transparency in process, even at the risk of some legal exposure.

At All Saints leaders could have talked to people about the policy that exists. They could have explained their regret that the letter of that policy had not been followed. They could also have explained that a singular troubling incident had occurred, which the senior pastor, the music director, and the governing board all concurred was egregious. They can say that the incident involved the safety of the youth without going into the specifics of the event.

Talk about the values of the congregation and how those values were honored in your process. Leaders can stress their attempts to preserve the core values of the congregation in the decisions that were made. Leaders can talk openly and honestly about the personal values struggle they engaged in while they made this very difficult decision, without sharing the details of the employee's situation. In Audrey's case leadership could talk about their interest in balancing the fair and equitable treatment of employees against the safety of the children and the need for a cohesive staff team.

Talk about the leaders who were involved in the decision. Let congregational members know which of their leaders had access to all of the details of the decision, not so they can pump those people for information, but so they know that some of their most trusted members were actively involved in the situation. In particular emphasize the checks and balances that existed through multiple levels of review to insure that the employee was treated fairly. At All Saints when people began to understand that leaders other than the music director were involved in Audrey's dismissal, they began to calm down.

Whenever possible, involve the terminated employee in a discussion about how his or her dismissal will be communicated. The dismissed employee is more likely to exit graciously if his or her concerns have been addressed regarding the communication of the dismissal. In Audrey's case, she wanted to be able to contact a few key families first before a general announcement was made. Church leaders may have had more control of the overall situation if they had allowed Audrey a few agreed upon contacts. Leaders may even have followed up one-on-one with those families after Audrey's contact to make sure that those families were hearing a balanced perspective about the situation.

If you are offering the dismissed employee a severance package, consider making a gracious departure a requisite to receiving the severance. You will probably want to seek legal help with crafting such an approach. You will need to give careful thought to the wording that describes what a gracious departure looks like. Never try to silence the dismissed employee by insisting on no contact. Members of your congregation are likely to receive that as a sign that the employee is being unfairly treated. However, you may want to place some limits on the type of contact considered acceptable and the type of information the employee is free to share about the dismissal.

Help people grieve and talk about their relationship with the terminated employee. This is particularly important for the long-term or much loved employee who is dismissed or the employee who is also a congregational member. Help people explore the changed nature of the relationship. Talk about what they should say and do if the employee seeks them out to triangulate, complain, or gossip about the situation. At All Saints a well-timed meeting between church leadership and the families that had participated in Audrey's ministry would have been well advised. Leaders could have helped those families develop an agreed upon response to Audrey's attempts at contact.

In the painful aftermath of employee termination, focusing on all of the things that you can talk about with the congregation will help to keep anxiety at a minimum.

Chapter 15

Staff Files

What Do I Keep and Why?

As a child Susan attended a parochial elementary school. Most of the children held great respect for the office of the principal. The principal's office was the place where all student discipline took place. Mysterious things were rumored to take place behind those closed doors, and none of them was good. One of the mysterious legends that she remembers permeated the school was the existence of a "permanent record" that was maintained for each student by the principal. This was not just any record. It was a *permanent* record, and it was said to hold all of one's deepest shortcomings and elementary school mistakes. If you were absent or tardy, it went into the permanent record. If you missed doing your homework one too many times, a permanent mark went on the record. Disrespect a teacher, and a very dark mark was attached to your name.

Susan has no idea what kind of records the school actually maintained on each child, but it is doubtful it was anywhere close to the kind of records the children kept in their imaginations. The frightening aspect of a permanent record was twofold. First, it did not appear that there was any way to undo something once it became part of the file. Something that appeared in the file actually was considered a part of one's character. Second, the child had no control over what apparently got recorded. Most of them imagined that by the time they reached high school, their days already would be numbered by the darkness of the record that would follow them.

We all can identify with the notion of the permanent record and the fearfulness of having someone record our worst shortcomings and foibles for all eternity. It is not remarkably unlike the kind of hysteria that goes on in workplace settings over what should be included in—or excluded from—a personnel file. Susan served as a human resource manager in a corporate setting for a number of years before finding her way into the world of congregations. The most frequent visits she received from employees during that time related to three basic topics: benefits questions, problems with performance evaluations, and requests to view their personnel records. We may have moved beyond our elementary notions of a permanent record that follows us from place to place, but the mystery of the personnel file still consumes us. The personnel record stands up there with our credit report rating and our record with the department of motor vehicles in forming a history of what we have done. It is no wonder that there is such sensitivity to what we put into it and how long documents are kept.

In the world of congregations, loftier notions of being in covenantal relationships with other people tend to replace understandings of work as a relationship governed by legal and union requirements. It is easy to think that people in congregations do not worry about such things—other than trying to be fair and to honor legal minimums. This may be a mistaken assumption. For example, Susan's conversation one day with a church employee whom we will call Karen reminded her of how important the permanence of the personnel file is—even in the mind of church employees.

Susan was working with a congregation that had ended its relationship with its previous pastor in troubled fashion. Several weeks into the assignment, Karen came into the office to talk about the absence of her personnel file. Apparently the previous pastor had taken a number of files that should have remained behind. One of them was Karen's personnel file. As they talked about the disappearance of Karen's file, Susan became aware of how violated Karen felt by the removal of her permanent employee record. Somehow it seemed to diminish the collective value of all the good work she had done for the church. Its absence created a hole in her sense of history as an employee.

Susan's encounter with Karen underscores the fact that the creation and maintenance of files about our relationship with staff members truly is a form of sacred trust. The thought and care that leaders put into the maintenance of people's records in ministry together is a reflection of the relationship itself. Taking time to create records that are reflective of the genuine nature of our relationship honors those relationships.

We see evidence of this kind of care in record keeping all throughout the Hebrew Scriptures, especially in the book of Numbers. The book of Numbers incorporates two military censuses that make special effort to outline the job responsibilities of various tribes and clans. The tasks that people performed, the assignment of their roles, and their responsibilities were recorded as part of the sacred story. Our congregations are a continuation of that ancient faith story, and we need to attend to our accounting of the story by documenting the work of our people with a similar kind of care.

Legal Issues

So what exactly are congregations supposed to keep in staff files and for how long? Much of that depends on the legal environment. There are many faith-based reasons for wanting to maintain good records, but the reality is that each congregation operates within legal parameters set forth by the government and judicatory systems in which we all operate. The nature of the files that are to be kept is most likely to take shape from state requirements and judicatory policies. Leaders will want to check on state laws and denominational policies before making any definitive choices about what to keep and how long to keep it.

Most of the legal issues concerning human resource files are related to issues of privacy. The Fourth Amendment to the U.S. Constitution guarantees protection from unreasonable search and seizure. The ability of a congregation—or its representatives—to search an employee's files without his or her permission might well violate that protection. In addition, the Fifth Amendment provides protection against self-incrimination, and if a congregation searches through an employee's personnel file and finds incriminating information, this action could be viewed as a violation of that protection.

The Privacy Act of 1974 requires federal agencies to open their personnel files for employee inspection. Furthermore, the law enables the employee to correct any incorrect or misleading information in those files and allows the employee to prevent the use of the information in those files for anything other than its original intent. These rights have not yet extended legally beyond the boundaries of federal agencies. Employment practices protecting those kinds of rights, however, have become mainstream.[1]

The Americans with Disabilities Act (ADA) provides that separate files must be maintained for medical records related to disabilities and the reasonable accommodation of those disabilities. These records are to be maintained in a separate, locked cabinet, apart from personnel files. Access to these files is limited to those supervisory personnel involved in the implementation of workplace accommodations. Random drug-screen information for employees in a drug-testing program also should be maintained in the medical file, as should information related to worker's compensation, the Family and Medical Leave Act (FMLA), and any leave-of-absence information regarding the same.

Under federal law, all employers—including the smallest congregations—must have a form on file that verifies the employment eligibility and identity of each employee. The Immigration Reform and Control Act requires all U.S. employers to complete the Employment Eligibility Verification Form (Form I-9) for all employees, including U.S. citizens.

Ethical Issues

Some of the legal restrictions in place that potentially limit the information a congregation can store about employees and how that information is used are noted above. These restrictions are likely to increase over time. In addition to the legal restrictions, however, there are a number of ethical considerations that should guide the design and use of personnel files.

Medical information related to the physical or emotional health of the employee probably should not be stored in the personnel file.

If a reason exists for you to maintain such information, store it separately with the ADA and FMLA information referred to above. Retaining such information in an employee file may encourage someone reviewing that file to use the information inappropriately in an employee decision. Additionally, the existence of the information could cause embarrassment or discomfort for an employee if it were made known later to a supervisor who had no need to know about the condition.

There is also the question of how long to retain documents in an employee file that pertain to disciplinary proceedings or progressive discipline if the employee's behavior has improved. People in faith communities believe in the power of redemption and reconciliation. If an employee has significantly turned around his or her behavior, at some point it is appropriate to consider expunging the prior problematic behavior from his or her record. A note about problematic behavior that is several years old will not hold validity in most legal proceedings if there has not been a repeat of the behavior in the interim. Leaders may want to consider establishing a rule that removes records of previous infractions after an acceptable expanse of time without relapse.

Checklist: What to Include in the Personnel File

An employee's personnel file should actually consist of three components:

- The employee's general file—described below, maintained by the personnel function.
- The employee's medical file—described above, maintained by the personnel function but separate from the general file.
- The employer's private file—consists of reference checks, credit checks, information regarding legal actions or complaints, notes about verbal conversations with the employee that precede formal written warnings, etc.; maintained by the employee's supervisor.

The employee's general file contains personnel documents that have a direct relation to the employee's job, such as licenses/certificates, performance evaluations, employment application, and records of salary changes.

Access to the general employee file should be limited only to those with an immediate management need to know. This typically would include the direct supervisor, head of staff, and members of the human relations or parish relations committee if the committee is involved in the direct oversight of employees. We recommend keeping the general employee file separate from the private and medical file.

The following checklist describes the documents that we recommend for inclusion in a general employee file, along with how long they ought to be maintained:

Contents	Retention Period
Hiring Documents	
Permanent: • signed application • resume • signed job description • offer letter • acceptance letter • signed ethics agreement (if required) • licenses/certificates (if required) • curriculum transcripts (if required)	Minimum of seven years after employee's departure. Some denominations recommend keeping these records indefinitely.
Temporary: • INS I-9 forms • emergency notification • updated job descriptions	Follow state guidelines (typically one to three years).

Contents	Retention Period
Performance Management Documents • salary contract and change notices • correspondence related to salary • changes in job classification • performance appraisals • education assistance • letters of recognition • staff service awards • attendance and absence records • applications and grants for sabbatical leave	Follow state guidelines (typically one to three years).
Disciplinary Documents • warning letters • disciplinary demotion or decrease in pay • suspension without pay • intent to dismiss • notice of dismissal	Until matter is concluded. Three years from time of incident if the problem behavior has been corrected.

The care that you demonstrate in creating and maintaining accurate personnel records will send an important message to your staff team about their worth and value. Haphazard record keeping devalues the contribution of staff members. Well-kept records support a culture of effectiveness.

Epilogue

The congregation had been large for quite some time. Tracing the history, one could see that average attendance was over one thousand in the 1970s. It was an earlier time in which people joined the church with a strongly formed consensus about what all congregations of this particular denomination did. The members (for there were only members—if you were a participant in those days with no interest in joining, you were considered to be a "bad member") came with a shared idea of their congregation already in mind. They agreed on how the congregation would worship, what the structure was to be like, what programs were to be provided, what missionaries were to be supported, when on Sunday evening the youth group would gather, and what the kids would do for their special activities during the year.

The senior pastor worked hard in those earlier years, no doubt about it. But his work was simpler and could be managed relationally. The senior pastor got to know the people and had personal relationships with the leaders. He (for the senior pastor was invariably a "he") was to work closely with the seventy-five people on the governing board and keep telling them what was important for the congregation to be working on. Building a stronger consensus within the large governing board would help keep the large church on track and stable. If more money was needed, the senior pastor was to go and talk personally with the wealthier active members. He was to build good relationships with the staff and keep them encouraged but not worry too much about directing their work, because everyone knew what was expected.

The relational style of leadership fit this earlier time very well since there were few differences and expectations to negotiate. The congregation learned how to get along quite well. Where there was a lack of structure or missing controls, the business manager stepped in and provided reports to the board to help them see what was missing. The business manager stepped in to offer the needed supervision and alignment to the quickly growing staff by requiring staff to begin to account for their time. He approved or rejected expenditures depending on whether the budget allowed the expense—or more to the point, depending on whether the business administrator thought what the staff person was doing was good.

This congregation had learned its relational leadership style early on when that style worked, and it had kept using the informal practices long after they were appropriate. No systems were built by which a small governing board could discern a future and set actual priorities that would move the congregation toward a clear future, directed by a shared vision. Staff were simply told, "Work hard, keep busy, and keep people happy." No systems were built for visioning or to align and supervise staff. Where there was lack of direction and priorities, the staff competed for resources and bristled against the misunderstood controls of the business manager. No systems of accountability were built by which the staff knew what they were to produce and what resources they had at their disposal. By the time a consultant was called in, staff were in small competing subgroups, several of them no longer talking to one another, with a deep division between the administrative staff and the program staff. They were in a contest to see who would be in control. The senior pastor continued to practice relational leadership and tried to deal with the situation by negotiating one-on-one with feuding staff to encourage them to treat one another better. He encouraged staff to avoid dealing directly with others where there was out and out conflict.

In an earlier day, the ideas in this book were not needed in large congregations. Informality and relationships ruled the day. Like every other part of North American life that can be assessed, life in large congregations has become increasingly complex over the years, now demanding formality and accountability—and the tools and structures to support this shift.

The senior clergy leadership of staff described in this book is different and requires practices that senior clergy of large congregations have not been taught. Curiously, many of the leaders in these congregations are more familiar with the practices outlined here than clergy are because they encounter a version of these practices and tools in their workplaces. These practices most familiar to laity, however, are often designed more appropriately to fit for-profit companies and nonprofit institutions. It has not occurred to many of these leaders that these same systems are needed in their churches because they too have learned to think of their congregations relationally. It is interesting to work with a personnel committee in one of these congregations where one or more of the committee members is a human resource director in a hospital, university, or business. The light quickly goes on in his or her mind when the issues are described, and the "of course" response follows quickly. These people who understand human resource management are amazingly helpful in supporting their senior clergy in building the necessary systems and practices. It is regularly part of Gil's practice as a consultant to encourage boards to form a personnel subgroup of a few of these people to work directly and continuously with the senior pastor in installing the new systems and practices.

Since large congregations are a relatively new phenomenon, the leadership of them is still being learned—and taught to others—by those who are doing it. This book is intended to support that learning. Like all good learning in a time of great change, the "answers" in this book will actually produce better questions for leaders to figure out, and in turn the leadership needed in our larger congregations will deepen. To that end we give thanks.

Notes

Introduction

1. Scott Thumma, Dave Travis, and Warren Bird, *Megachurches Today: 2005 Summary of Research Findings*, Hartford Institute for Religion Research, http://hirr.hartsem.edu/megachurch/megastoday2005_summaryreport.html (accessed June 25, 2007).
2. Mark Chaves, *How Do We Worship?* (Herndon, VA: Alban, 1999), 9.
3. Ibid., 8.
4. General Board of Global Ministries, United Methodist Church, "Top 200 United Methodist Churches by Worship Attendance, 2003," May 18, 2005, research@gbgm-umc.org.

Chapter 1: People Are Resources for Ministry

1. Eliza G. C. Collins and Mary Anne Devanna, *The Portable MBA* (New York: Wiley, 1990), 219.
2. Jim Collins, *Good to Great: Why Some Companies Make the Leap . . . and Others Don't* (New York: Harper Business, 2001), 45.
3. Marcus Buckingham and Curt Coffman, *First Break All the Rules: What the World's Greatest Managers Do Differently* (New York: Simon and Schuster, 1999), 59.
4. Douglas McGregor, *The Human Side of Enterprise* (New York: McGraw-Hill, 1960).
5. Marvin Weisbord, *Productive Workplaces: Organizing and Managing for Dignity, Meaning, and Community* (San Francisco: Berrett-Koehler, 1993), 114.

6. Buckingham and Coffman, *First Break All the Rules*, 201.

7. Peter Block, *Stewardship: Choosing Service over Self-Interest* (San Francisco: Berrett-Kohler, 1993), 147–51.

8. Buckingham and Coffman, *First Break All the Rules*, 27–28.

9. Collins and Devanna, *The Portable MBA*, 220.

Chapter 3: The Importance of Outcomes

1. Gil Rendle and Alice Mann, *Holy Conversations: Strategic Planning as a Spiritual Practice for Congregations* (Herndon, VA: Alban, 2003), 3–6.

2. Arthur Koestler, *The Ghost in the Machine* (New York: Macmillan, 1967), 55, 76.

3. "A Brief History of Mission San Luis Rey Retreat Center," prepared by Mission San Luis Rey Retreat Center, Oceanside, CA, www.sanluisrey.org.

Chapter 4: The Critical Job Description

1. John M. Ivancevich and Michael T. Matteson, *Organizational Behavior and Management* (Boston: Irwin, 1993), 302–7.

2. An important work in this field is R. L. Kahn, D. M. Wofe, R. P. Quinn, and J. D. Snoek, *Organizational Stress: Studies in Role Conflict and Ambiguity* (New York: Wiley, 1964), 12–26.

3. Adele Margrave and Robert Gorden, *The Complete Idiot's Guide to Performance Appraisal* (New York: Penguin Putnam, 2001), 63–65.

4. These core competencies are adapted from Michael M. Lombardo and Robert W. Eichinger, *The Career Architect Portfolio Sort Cards*, Lominger Limited, 1996, Version 7.1a.

Chapter 5: Hiring Right to Manage Easier

1. Jim Collins, *Good to Great: Why Some Companies Make the Leap . . . and Others Don't* (New York: Harper Business, 2001), 13.

2. Lori Davila and Louise Kursmark, *How to Choose the Right Person for the Right Job Every Time* (New York: McGraw-Hill, 2005), 11–14.

3. Ibid., 42–43.

Chapter 6: Supervision as Performance Management

1. William Oncken Jr. and Donald Wass, "Management Time: Who's Got the Monkey?" *Harvard Business Review*, November-December 1974 (reprint #74607).

2. Peter Block, *Stewardship: Choosing Service over Self-Interest* (San Francisco: Berrett-Kohler, 1993), 147–60.

3. Thomas Cooley, "Charge to the Students," Graduation Exercises at Stern School of Business, New York University, Madison Square Garden, NY, May 11, 2005.

4. C. Jeff Woods, *User Friendly Evaluation* (Bethesda, MD: Alban, 1995), 68–69.

5. Marcus Buckingham and Curt Coffman, *First Break All the Rules: What the World's Greatest Managers Do Differently* (New York: Simon and Schuster, 1999), 47–49.

6. F. J. Roethlisberger and W. J. Dickson, *Management and the Worker* (Cambridge: Harvard University Press, 1939).

7. Thomas J. Peters and Robert H. Waterman, *In Search of Excellence: Lessons from America's Best Run Companies* (New York: Warner, 1993).

Chapter 7: Delegation

1. Mindtools, Ltd., http://www.mintoolds.com/stress/workoverload/delegation.htm (accessed August 2005).

2. Gary Yukl, *Leadership in Organizations*, 4th ed. (Upper Saddle River, NJ: Prentice Hall, 1998), 133–40.

3. Adapted from by Ken Blanchard, Patricia Zigarmi, and Drea Zigarmi, *Leadership and the One Minute Manager* (New York: William Morrow, 1995).

4. Ken Blanchard, John Carlos, and Alan Randolph, *The Three Keys to Empowerment* (San Francisco: Berrett-Kohler, 1999), 24.

5.   Yukl, *Leadership*, 142–45.

Chapter 8: Helping Staff Negotiate Their Needs

1.   Lawrence Porter and Bernard Mohr, eds., *Reading Book for Human Relations Training* (Arlington, VA: National Training Laboratories, 1982), 68–71.
2.   Peter Steinke, *How Your Church Family Works: Understanding Congregations as Emotional Systems* (Herndon, VA: Alban Institute, 1993), 15–19.
3.   John Sherwood and John Scherer, "A Model for Couples: How Two Can Grow Together," *Small Group Behavior* 6, no. 1 (February 1975): 11–29.
4.   Ibid., 15.
5.   Ibid., 17.
6.   Ibid., 22.
7.   Ronald Heifetz, *Leadership without Easy Answers* (Cambridge: Belknap Press of Harvard University Press, 1994), 104.

Chapter 9: Performance Evaluation

1.   "What Our Members Say about Evaluation," *Congregations* 28, no. 2 (March-April 2002): 27.
2.   W. Edward Demming, *Out of the Crisis* (Cambridge, MA: MIT Press, 1982), 102.
3.   Marcus Buckingham, *The One Thing You Need to Know: . . . About Great Managing, Great Leading, and Sustained Individual Success* (New York: Free Press, 2005), 101–2.
4.   Donald Clifton and James K. Harter, "Investing in Strengths," in *Positive Organizational Scholarship* (San Francisco: Berrett-Kohler, 2003), 111–21.
5.   Harry Levinson, "Management by Whose Objectives?" *Harvard Business Review*, July-August 1970.
6.   Jill Hudson, *Evaluating Ministry: Principles and Processes for Clergy and Congregations* (Herndon, VA: Alban Institute, 1992), 6–7.

7. *Theological and Theoretical Foundations for Evaluating Ministry*, a pamphlet prepared by the Division of Ordained Ministry, Board of Higher Education, and Ministry of the United Methodist Church (Nashville, 1990).

8. Ken Langdon and Christina Osborne, *Essential Managers: Performance Reviews* (New York: DK Publishing, 2001), 8–9.

9. Thomas Gilbert, *Human Competence: Engineering Worthy Performance* (New York: McGraw-Hill, 1978), 88.

10. Frederick Herzberg, Bernard Mausner, and Barbara Bloch Snyderman, *The Motivation to Work* (New York: Wiley, 1959).

11. J. Stacy Adams, "Toward an Understanding of Equity," *Journal of Abnormal and Social Psychology*, November 1963, 422–36.

Chapter 10: Staff Team Design

1. Judith Gordon, *Organizational Behavior: A Diagnostic Approach*, 6th ed. (Upper Saddle River, NJ: Prentice-Hall, 1999), 369.

2. John Ivancevich and Michael Matteson, *Organizational Behavior and Management* (Homewood, IL: Irwin, 1993), 510.

3. These questions are adapted from the original work of Michael Goold and Andrew Campbell, "Do You Have a Well-Designed Organization?" *Harvard Business Review*, March 2002, 5–11.

4. Lyle Schaller, *The Multiple Staff and the Larger Church* (Nashville: Abingdon, 1980).

5. Gary L. McIntosh, *Staff Your Church for Growth: Building Team Ministry in the 21st Century* (Grand Rapids: Baker, 2000).

Chapter 11: Staff Meetings

1. Gordon Kingsley, "The President as Bard," *AGB Reports*, July-August 1987, 18–21.

2. Walter Wink, *Unmasking the Powers* (Philadelphia: Fortress Press, 1986), 69–86.

Chapter 12: Dealing with Difficult Staff Behavior

1. Edwin Friedman, *Friedman's Fables* (New York: Guilford, 1990), 25.

2. M. Scott Peck, *The Different Drummer: Community Making and Peace* (New York: Simon and Schuster, 1987), 86.

3. Ronald A. Heifetz and Donald L. Laurie, "The Work of Leadership," *Harvard Business Review*, January-February 1997, 128.

4. Thomas H. Davenport and Laurence Prusak, *Working Knowledge: How Organizations Manage What They Know* (Boston: Harvard Business School Press, 2000), 90.

5. John Guaspari, *I Know It When I See It: A Modern Fable about Quality* (New York: AMACOM, 1983).

6. Gil Rendle, *Behavioral Covenants in Congregations: A Handbook for Honoring Differences* (Herndon, VA: Alban Institute, 1999), 19–20.

7. Stephen Carter, *Civility: Manners, Morals, and the Etiquette of Democracy* (New York: Basic Books, 1998).

8. Rendle, *Behavioral Covenants*, 50–51.

9. Ibid., resource section: Resource I.

10. Kenneth Mitchell, *Multiple Staff Ministries* (Philadelphia: Westminster Press: 1988), 135.

Chapter 13: Dealing with Poor Performance or Terminating Employment

1. Associated Press interview, 1997.

2. Jim Collins, *Good to Great: Why Some Companies Make the Leap . . . and Others Don't* (New York: Harper Business, 2001), 41.

3. Ibid., 56.

4. While progressive discipline is a common human resource practice in organizations, the authors are particularly indebted to Elma Benavides, associate vice president for human resources at Southwestern University in Texas for her help in working with these issues in congregational settings. The steps of progressive

discipline and their use, as well as the descriptions of the steps, are heavily borrowed from Ms. Benavides's practice with and training of managers.

Chapter 15: Staff Files

1. Angelo DeNisis and Ricky Griffin, *Human Resource Management* (New York: Houghton Mifflin, 2001), 534–35.